A
Page
in
Time

By
James B. Miller

A narrative of the Wyoming Valley, 1778

A Page in Time

Copyright 2010 by James B. Miller

This book may be ordered **online or at any fine bookseller**.

ISBN:1456315323
EAN-13:9781456315320

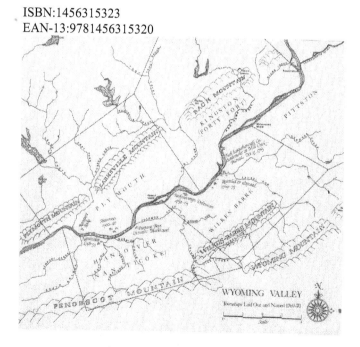

Dedication

This book is dedicated to my father, my daughter Angela, my grandson Cayleb, and to our common ancestor, Moses Brown.

Author's note

This narrative is based on fact. All people portrayed in these pages actually lived and the places are real. It is based on Moses Brown's(the author's ancestor) ordeal before and after the Battle of Wyoming, in the Wyoming Valley, in what is now Northern Pennsylvania, but then Connecticut. It has been thoroughly researched and the author hopes it promotes an understanding of the people living at the birth of this great nation. For it is his fondest wish they not be forgotten, never.

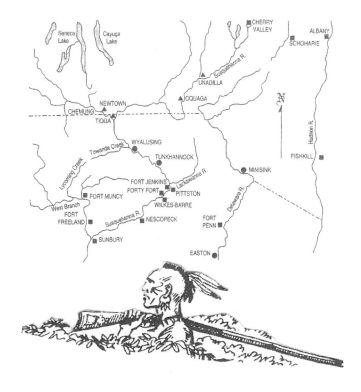

Chapter One

Some say not everyone held the torch of freedom high, well I don't know about that, just to say as boy of Wyoming at the time of the *Revolution,* almost every heart there thudded to the beat of the new nation. There were few, very few, whose cold hearts did not, the hated *Tories*, and in the end I must say their treachery was unmatched. Many a patriots' bones still lay on the battlefield at Wyoming bearing stark testimony of that fact.

It is after many years I sit to write this, after all the hubbub has faded with time. Certainly there are a few old veterans still about, a distant reminder of times past; times now romanticized in the shadows of the memories of those aged fellows, but as a lad, those times did shine with a certain glare. The shadows of fear which also inhabited the time now lay forgotten, but at the time, I tell you, they were very real. Thus is why I take up my pen to tell of the times now swept with glory in the memory of this burgeoning and blessed nation.

So sit back as I, in the light of a roaring fire by the hearth, and let your imagination glow with the memory of that time. Such a time comes very rarely in the slow march of time. A time ushering great change, and thus great fear, enticing emotions in our people which still live, and haunt the memories of this nation to this day.

To start, one not born of the time may ask just where was this place called Wyoming, though I assure at the time its name rolled off the tongues of such men as Benjamin Franklin, George Washington, John Adams, and Thomas Jefferson, with a familiarity the same as Philadelphia or Boston. For it lay on the southern door of the Great Iroquois Confederacy, the mightiest and strongest Indian Confederacy thus known on the North American continent. From its place of importance it checked the Iroquois from flowing freely down to Philadelphia and beyond. Though one may doubt it now, it was at the time of very great importance, but tainted at the same time. For there were some of the Penn faction of Pennsylvania whom also lay claim to it, though it was clearly in Connecticut's Land

4

Grant of 1662; which predated the Penn's Charter by some nineteen years. The Penns, a most powerful family of the time, disputed our rightful claim only after we began to settle the land, like a spoiled child wanting a neglected toy which they had disregarded because they saw someone else take pleasure in it, whom recognized its true charm. But that is a festering story of another time, which still draws angst in both the Pennamite's and Yankee's heart after all these past years. So, I tell you at the time of the Revolution Wyoming was known as the area from Tioga Point, now Athens, Pennsylvania, all the way down the mighty Susquehanna River to Nescopeck, Pennsylvania. Athens is a great place with a wealth of unknown and neglected history, named after the birth place of democracy by Wyoming settlers split from their brethren about Wilkes-Barre after the last Pennamite-Yankee War just after the Revolution.

These spirited settlers, known at the time as *Wild Yankees,* were led by men whom most fervently held the cause of Wyoming and their rightful Connecticut claim sacred, not to be denied by anyone, for their blood lay in the land, and the sweat of many year's toil. Their love for Wyoming and what the nation represented was boundless and limitless. Thus the hearts of many a true patriot lay there, men such as Judge John Jenkins, feared and despised by the Iroquois and British at Niagara, once captured and taken to a festering hole of misery within its walls by the hated and betraying Tories, and John Franklin, thrice wounded in the defense of his country in the Pennamite Wars and the glorious Revolution. Judge Obadiah Gore, General Simon Spalding, William Judd, and John Swift, a *Wild Yankee* who rose to the rank of Brigadier General in the War of 1812 and was killed leading his troops in defense of his nation in that war, called Athens their blessed home. A place harboring such fervent patriot's blood should be revered, and at the time of this writing still is, thank God.

But on with the story, for the story belongs to all from Wilkes-Barre to Athens, and I hope the two reconcile their differences and unite as they once did at the birth of this nation, for such people of like mind should, but I fear this wound to never heal, and to be passed from generation to generation so long the reason for the angst shall be forgotten, but not the emotion, which seems to live beyond all rational memory. I already see it among the remnants of the native tribes, loyal to the American cause at the time, whom are chastised at this time and relegated to the most menial and degrading parts of our society by a false prejudice born of another time. All that is remembered is the horror of that battlefield at Wyoming, the so-called massacre, where Native Americans whom had once called the people of Wyoming friend, along with the traitorous Tories, slaughtered those taking up arms against them. As I said, the emotion sheers into the memory the hate; but the reason of the hate is lost in time. Perhaps we should look to the reasons, and thus reject the hate cursing a people whose ancestors had nothing to do with it, but as I said, remained loyal to we Americans. But man is not perfect, is he? Perhaps that is why the most educated of men preach to us to think instead of just reacting, for if a man thinks, he must react, and in that expose his false prejudices, thus enabling him to shun them and be a better man, one which I hope he aspires to be.

Wyoming in 1778 was a beautiful place, before the hated war touched it, boasting a fine green in Wilkes-Barre, mills, stores, rich farms, and many uncultivated acres just waiting for the plow, and vast, virgin forests. All seemed right and well, for the Pennamites no longer bothered us, nor did we bother them, both uniting by pleas from Congress to suspend our differences until after the war in which we both shared an undying belief. I remember many a blissful day, before the Indian troubles, when we fished the rivers and swam in the creeks, unfettered by any concerns, but just lived in the day, a day shinning brighter all the time. Only the threat of the cloud hanging over us from Fort Niagara, that bastion of the hated Tories, whom endlessly tried to provoke our peaceful Indian neighbors against us, hovered over our optimistic heads like a foreboding dark thundercloud on the far distant horizon. A heavy cloud, but far away, nonetheless, and most folks prayed that's where it would remain. As time proved later, it would not.

So it was in this spring of 1777 that I as a young boy thought the paradise I lived in to remain the pristine jewel set amidst the wilderness forever. Though others talked about the starving times before and such, it sounded to me to be nothing but a fairytale, for of all of my short life I had known nothing but plenty and good cheer, save an engagement with the Pennamites a few years before which still glared in some people's memory. Besides, what is a youth to care but how warm the river is, or where the best holes for fishing are, or what wonders Mathis Hollenback brought up the river in his fully loaded bateaux for his store? This always brought a wonder to I and my friends, and upon hearing the call of his approach, we would race across the green by the fort to gaze in wonder at the treasures. If the landing be made across the river we would race across in canoes or rafts, and on rare occasions when the river was low, swim across it, a test of stamina to see whom reached the far shore first. Such were the concerns of boys in those days. Oh, such times were simple and pure. Such times of ease and joy.

This one fine day, with the sky bright, crisp, and clear in early spring, a fine hubbub had all the grown up folk in a tizzy. We all, most everyone that is, followed the call to the Nathan Denison house near Kingston, on the west side of the river, which I lived not far from, so the men could discuss a most urgent matter. Us young boys, clad only in our knee britches and loose fitting linen shirts, as was the custom when the warm days arrived, ran barefoot across the yard in front of the house, playing tag and what not as our mothers stood just outside the front door of the house whispering between themselves about something the men discussed inside the house. For all the prominent men of the valley answered the call, as they did at the muster for the militia and such, and sat dressed in their finest inside the hot house, discussing important matters while fanning themselves with their hats.

I always recall, and will never forget, one booming voice, our hero's voice us boys called it, which always rose above the others. I remember hearing it that day long ago as we played, just as I had caught young Jabez Elliot by the door and tagged him. Being a bit older he seemed embarrassed by the shaking heads of the women folk around, but he was always one to play, no matter what age.

"I got you," I called in triumph, scampering away to avoid Jabez's long reach. He twirled around, totally surprised, and suddenly got caught up in the voices of the serious men echoing through a near window. He listened intently to the voices until my taunts beckoned him away from them.

"I'll get you Little Mose!" he said, "liken I would a Mohawk!" The reference to the feared Iroquois brought a gasp from some near ladies, whom promptly scolded the sprinting boy running pell-mell after me towards nearby Abraham's Creek. Coming upon its steep bank I lost all control, slipping and sliding down the leave-strewn bank with a howling Jabez at my heels. It was then we heard it. The great booming voice announcing that as long as he stood no savage or Tory would ever step foot in Wyoming without being strung up at the end of a rope. It silenced all around, even us boys, who twirled around and scrambled back up the bank, willingly forgetting our game for the sake of witnessing the loud man of Hanover, Lazarus Stewart, of the infamous Paxtang Rangers, Indian haters each and every one, and by my recollection the first ones I ever heard spout most frequently their creed-the only good Indian was a dead one!

A braggart he may have been, but he had proved himself brave in many a battle and skirmish with Pennamite and Indian alike, and thus earned his bragging rights, so none protested against him. For staunch men of character where needed in those days, and much was forgiven of a brave man.

Reaching the side window all of us boys sat breathlessly below it, intensely listening to our hero's voice command all the others. Jabez, along with my younger brother Will and I, even found the nerve to peek our eyes just over the open window sill.

Lazarus stood tall among the others, pacing back and forth and spouting his beliefs on the matter at hand. "No," he said, "I do not discount the veracity of the report, though brought to us by a Pennamite from Penn's Creek. They are our brethren now. Our enemies, the Mohawks, Tories, and such, are now their enemies, too!" He tilted back his head and gazed down his long nose to the man standing before him clasping his hat in his hands to his front. The man nodded and Lazarus put a hand to the black neck stock under his short collar as if such proper dress felt most uncomfortable to him. He was a fine figure of a man and upon reflection I can see why all the boys of Wyoming liked him. He was a true frontiersman, for good or bad, he always spoke his mind, no matter whom it might offend. He showed his allegiance to the frontier by always wearing his black hunting shirt, despite he at the time being the Lieutenant Colonel of the militia regiment, duly elected by his peers. Most officers, such as Nathan Denison, standing by his side and Colonel of the Militia Regiment, the *Twenty Fourth Connecticut Regiment,* wore a fine regimental, as it was called at the time, of brown fabric with red facings, the colors of the Connecticut regiments. Lazarus would have none of it, a true individual to the end.

Glancing over to his staunch friend Denison pacing near the hearth, he ran his hand gently through his fine black shoulder-length hair to put a few wild strands which had come loose from the black ribbon tying it back into place. No one spoke while he considered his words, each waiting to hear where the brash man would take the conversation next. After straightening his hair, he strode back towards the center of the room, gesturing to a small desk in the corner of the room. "There yonder," he said, "lies the letter written to John Pickard of Putnam, by the Tunkhannock Creek, by his cousin Nicholas, a known Tory, warning John to vacate his land from the storm of Indians and Tories planning to descend upon our homes come spring! I find it bold and most pretentious to say the least, gentlemen!" A series of huzzas answered the man. It was all us boys could do to hold our tongues as not to be discovered, for we wished to huzza for our hero the most of any. "I say we dispatch men at once to apprehend said men, for I hear Nicholas may be about the Tunkhannock Creek by no less of a truer patriot than Zebulon Marcy of those parts! We must find the truth of the matter! The Committee of Safety must act!" Canes thumped on the floor and fine men, young and old alike, all huzzaed again.

Lazarus, content he had said his piece, slowly eased his way to a corner, silently trying to mix in as one of the crowd, but the eyes of the men shinning about him forbade it. He nodded to each of them and spread his hand towards his friend Colonel Denison, who gave a slight bow as he strode to the center of the floor.

A hand to the back of our necks promptly pulled us away from the window, and away from the sight of our hero. We scurried and all scattered at once, melting into the crowd before the militia man's boot caught our backsides. Coming to a stop by a great tree near the Wyoming Road stretching across the plain before the house, we all gathered, forming an impromptu circle to discuss the matter as staunchly and earnestly as our elders.

"I say we march on the Tory rats at Tioga Point!" Jabez said, standing tall and jutting his chest, no doubt portraying himself as our hero Stewart. All of the boys huzzaed without a single voice in objection, much as our elders had done.

Jabez nodded at each and every one of us and yelled "Form up, ye men of Wyoming! For now we march against the Tory rascals and their savage allies! It'll be their hair that's missing in the end! Not ours!"

All of the boys formed a hasty line as we had seen our fathers, brothers, and uncles do every fortnight at militia drill. Jabez, at thirteen the eldest and tallest of the boys, marched up and down the line, inspecting each of the rough farm boys with a glaring eye. "No! The Tories and Indians haven't one chance against such men!" he announced, repeating what he had heard time and time again from our elders. "I would place one of ours against thrice their number!"

Us boys all jutted our chests in response and stood tall in our wavy line, pretending to shoulder our stick firelocks and stand at attention. On the command forward we all moved together before a call came from behind, "There they are just ahead, the Mohawk Brant and that Tory Indian Butler!" With a simultaneous yell we all rushed forwards at our imagined enemies, screaming like banshees and firing our make believe stick firelocks as fast as our lips could sputter the sound. "Tory's beware! Mohawks beware! You've tread your last when you durst step on Wyoming soil!" we screamed. "Show ye heads if ye dare to the brave Continental Sons of Liberty!"

Such was our spirit in those days long past, both young and old, man and woman, and it seemed to fill the air, strong, resilient and brave. Oh what times, oh what a place!

Chapter Two

It was well after sunset, but we sat down to sup just the same, being held up so by the long meeting at the Denison house. I and my brother scampered onto the porch near our grandfather, Isaac Bennett, whom we stayed with seeing how Pa went with the two Independent Companies raised by Congress for the war from Wyoming. Pa had left almost a year ago and had fought in many a battle, at Millstone, Bound Brook, and latter on at Brandywine, Germantown, the mud fort, and White Marsh, before holing up with General Washington at Valley Forge, there to be picked along with my uncle Rufus Bennett to serve on Washington's own lifeguard, quite a honor, I am told, though somehow Rufus got out of it a couple of months later and his dear friend Ira Stephens, a personal aid to General Washington, after suffering an illness, did also, rejoining the Independent Companies under Captains Ransom and Durkee, who were two Seven Years War veterans whom had been appointed captains of the companies. From later letters Pa wrote home he longed to be released from the honor and rejoin the companies, for he would hear of the threats of war against Wyoming, and wished and prayed only to return and defend his home, the reason the companies had been ordered to be formed in the first place. But General Washington took a personal shine to him, so there he stayed, honored and befuddled at the same time. Come August 1778, when his time was up, he swore to come home and he did. The greater country mattered he said, but at the same time his smaller country, as he called Wyoming, needed him too. He loved Ma and always at the end of his letters had swooning praises for her, his dear Lois, and for his two boys, I and Will. He always wrote that I was the man of the family, and despite my age, I had to look out for Ma and my younger brother in his stead, though he always told me to mind and pay heed to Grandpa.

"You boys just sit still and rest your bones fer a spell," Grandpa now said, easing back in his rocker brought all the way from Connecticut. "Your Ma and Grandma will have victuals ready soon." he added, easing back in his rocker and bringing forth his long clay pipe. Fingering some tobacco from his pouch he looked down to us, watching our eager eyes to see just whom he would send for a spill from the spill box by the hearth to light his pipe. He had made it a game and each of us boys competed for the honor.

"Will," he finally said, looking down at the full bowl of his pipe, "fetch me a spill."

Will spurted up despite my hands tugging him down in a moment of jealousy and spurted through the cabin door, announcing to Ma his mission to fetch Grandpa's spill so's to light his pipe. I collapsed down in defeat on the porch again, folding my arms against my Grandpa's gaze.

"Don't fret son," he said. "You'll have your turn. The world always turns, if you don't get what you want this day, there's always the next."

"I miss Pa," I suddenly blurted out, not intentionally wanting to hurt Grandpa's feelings, but boys can be cruel when they feel they are cheated.

"Your Pa has important business to attend to," Grandpa said, seeming to miss the gist of my words. "He'll be back when he can, that I grant you boy, for he loves you all, and don't you ever fer doubt it none, young'un."

"I don't Grandpa," I said, watching Will triumphantly return with a shaving of curled wood from a special wood plane held up in his hands, carefully stepping as not to upset the glowing end of it.

"Why thank you, dear Will," Grandpa said, gently relieving him of his prize. "Mighty fine of you indeed." He put the lit end of the spill to the bowl of his pipe and took a long draw. Exhaling a long trail of smoke, he eased back in his chair. Shaking the spill out in his fingers, he tossed it to the ground just as two people approached the porch from the trail.

"Well, land sakes," he said, nodding his head. "It's good to see you John, and you too, dear Elizabeth."

"I hope it's no great intrusion upon your hospitality, but seeing how Elizabeth here's with child, we decided to take you up on your offer to stay the night," the tall man said, slowly removing his wide-brimmed slouch hat. "Our cabin is a ways off up in Exeter, and the meeting took so long and all."

"No need to say no more, lad," Grandpa said, leaning forwards in his rocker, "you both are always welcomed her, anytime."

"Well, once again, I thank you just the same," John said, nodding to us two wide-eyed boys staring up to him.

"And I thank you as well," Elizabeth said, taking John's hand to help her up the steps to the porch.

"Elizabeth Murphy?" Ma's voice called from inside the cabin. 'Is that you I hear, and you also, dear John?" She appeared through the door, wiping her hands on her apron before either could respond. She smiled and ushered Elizabeth through the door to a chair by the table, nodding and smiling at her handsome young husband.

"Mrs. Brown, Ma'am," John said with a courtly bow of his head. "As I was telling your father here, we decided to take you up on your offer to stay the night, seeing what a way Elizabeth is in and all. I thank you most kindly."

"Why of course," Ma said, "and you are certainly most welcome. You're welcome to come in and sit a spell or stay out here with the men folk enjoying the fresh spring air, for it has been such a long time coming this year."

"That it has, Mrs. Brown, that it has."

"Oh please, call me Lois, it would be a honor for me to be called by my first name as long as we're in polite company, you being such a fine strapping man and all." She looked up to the heavens afar and seemed to pray. "It has been so long since I've seen my dear Moses, I pray for him every chance I get."

"Yes, Mrs., uh, Lois that is."

"John don't be so coy," Elizabeth said from her chair. "We are among friends."

14

"Yes, I know Elizabeth."

"We have boiled pudding," Mother suddenly said, causing eyes to roll to the subject already dividing many households in Wyoming. It had become the high philosophical subject among many a sewing circle. The controversy being among the women whether to cook their boiled pudding the old fashioned English way with fine wheat flour and suet, or simply with finely ground yellow maize, the new way, the American way. This division struck a mighty cord in the women's hearts and had struck up many arguments which tore asunder many a long-standing relationship. Only through the intervention of the reverend preaching about simple human survival, compared to simple human foolishness, had the issue been resolved, or simply not spoken of anymore. Many whispers still passed in quiet corners in some homes among like-minded people favoring one side or the other, but there the issue remained, from the simple exposure of the foolish subject through the good reverend. Food, a necessity, need not cause such a silly division among the people when greater threats breathed down our necks, the good reverend plainly stated; and rightly so.

Will and I even sat hushed, causing mother to cast a coy smile and announce, "We cook ours with maize," before simply turning toward the door, finding her way back to her boiled pudding.

"Frankly," John said quietly to Grandfather, "I take my pudding either way, for a man's taste holds no bearing over his politics, I hope!"

Grandfather let a sly smile raise his jowls and let out a chuckle. "Aye to that, my friend," he said on a long exhale of smoke. "Aye to that!"

John then looked all about Grandpa's fine porch, nodding to my Grandfather's keen eye.

"It's an idea from the Africans put to building houses, a porch is," Grandfather explained. "A right fine one."

A call to supper brought us all to the table, each

casting a wary eye to the bundle holding the boiled pudding, but all held their tongue. Wyoming had enough troubles, what with the growing British and Indian threat at our door. So, the boiled pudding controversy stayed where in belonged, in the dark corners of the cabins and in certain petty people's hearts.

One of the mighty warriors of the
"Six Nations".

Chapter Three

As with all places on this jewel we call earth, even when one has found paradise something always comes by the way to taint it, as if sent by the hand of God to remind complacent folks of his existence. Such was this terrible time.

I remember hearing the whispers among my Grandpa and his friends passing by of something which clearly shot the fear of God into them. With widening eyes they would speak in a far corner, out of earshot of the children and women folk, as not to cause any undue panic or fear among them. It was the man's way to protect the so-called weaker of his flock from any business which might cause them distress. Thus, we watched the wave descend with each new visit of a friend, some passing just quick enough to bend down from their horses and whisper to my Grandpa before scampering on to spread the news upriver. The news, the terrible news, interrupted church, the work in the fields, fishing, coon hunting, and every other aspect of regular life-the dreaded *pox!*

This day, Grandpa, knowing the word had now passed from a mere rumor to absolute fact as the sick culprit returning from a recent trip to Philadelphia had died, gathered us all by the hearth and sat back in his rocker, his eyes aglow with dread. "It's come, it has," he simply said. "The *pox,* carried to us from Philadelphia, no less." He rubbed his tired chin and gazed about with a far away look as if witnessing some horror in the future playing out in his mind.

Grandma immediately looked down to us children, her jewels on earth, and scooped us up in her arms in a great hug. Mother stood wiping her hands on her apron from her ever present duty of cooking over the hearth and stared in shock at Grandpa.

"Now don't be getting all in a tizzy now," he said, shaking way the far away look. "They's setting up pest-houses in each township, back off the roads, a half mile respectfully. Wise and energetic souls are at work to lessen the effects of this plague, and I have faith in their actions, I do." He looked to Grandma clutching her precious jewels and to his blank-eyed daughter. "Doctors Gustin and Hooker Smith will work their way through the pest-houses, one starting downriver and the other up, until all the children are inoculated." He smiled down to us children but it did little to ease our angst, for we had been told to always avoid the mere mention of the word *pox*, let alone the pestilence itself. It ignited a terror in both of us. I durst say as I saw the little tears start to streaking down Will's face, they caused no less than a torrent to start pouring from my own eyes.

Mother, upon hearing her crying children, immediately bent down and joined in our great hug with Grandma. It seemed to shake her through and through. "You'll be fine, my darlings, don't you fret," she said. "But you must promise to stay close to home and if you see anybody passing, I don't care who, you get yourselves inside and you pull in the latch string! You hear?"

"Yes Ma," we both muttered through our quivering lips, feeling as if all the world had suddenly changed.

"She's right, my fine strong lads," Grandpa said with a half smile which barley masked his true concern and fear. "I've arranged for the children to be inoculated on the morrow, one of the first, in the old Foster cabin back off the road over by the fort," he said to our mother.

"Oh dear Isaac, has it spread far?" Grandma asked.

Grandpa scratched his head and leaned back in his rocking chair, seeming surprised the men had effectively kept the word from the gossip circles; a great feat indeed, knowing the women of Wyoming. He seemed to draw faith from that success alone. "It was carried by one of our most respected citizens returned from Philadelphia, he took sick and died yesterday, God rest his soul," Grandpa said, seeming proud he knew the first word about something for a change. "But it's not spread far yet, to but a few families, in fact. We shall quarantine as to prevent further spread, so the sewing circles, quilting bees, and such will have to be curtailed until such time as the threat has passed."

"Of course," Grandma said. "One needs lips to spread the middling words of the day, and there are no lips from the grave, save our Lord."

Grandpa nodded and asked of our stores, to which both Grandma and Mother said were ample for a fortnight, then we would need flour, salt, and such, but Grandfather assured them the danger should pass by then. If not, we could go to Hollenback's store, but only there, for it would be months before the true danger totally passed.

The weight of this suddenly hit both Grandma and Mother like a ton of brick. They both cast a rolling eye all along the cabin's walls. Growing pale, they looked to the greased-paper window in the far wall and sighed, no doubt reflecting on how we all had been cooped up all winter. Now, just as spring had arrived, they faced another bout of isolation. It did drain both women so. I felt such a great pity. My tears ceased and I turned to comfort them, feeling all the stronger watching Will still sobbing on Mother's lap.

"Well," Grandpa said, rising to offer the crestfallen women what comfort he could offer. "Leastways we shan't expect any attack from the Tories or Indians once they catch word of this, hear tell Denison had sent word of it already to Ester and that lot about Tioga Point," he said. "We'll be safe another season and by then they may just give up on their ill-advised plan, I durst say." Recognizing his words did little to relieve their angst, Grandpa turned to his own solace and sat back down in his rocker, lighting his pipe in the sudden gloom blanketing the cabin.

It would be a long spring indeed, and a long sleepless night for us children as visions of the horrid pest-house danced in our worried minds. Oh, to trade one pestilence for another did not seem a bargain made in heaven, but in hell alone.

The next morning we rose to Coward's crow. Coward being the name bestowed upon our rooster by Grandpa after many facing-offs with the fine white rooster. Grandfather seemed to enjoy his combat with the bird. Many a time I would see him around the corner of the cabin near the chicken coop staring down the proud bird, which would always end with Coward puffing his feathers out on his wings, apparently to make himself seem larger to his resilient foe. Then he would dart towards my laughing and taunting Grandfather, whom pushed it aside as it tried to spur or peck him with a long stick or simply his boot, gloating and pronouncing him a coward in his failed attempt to attack.

When some so-called friendly Indians still lived about us, before they suddenly all left one day in early spring a year before the summer of the massacre, one, named Anthony Turkey, upon visiting Grandfather would show great enjoyment from their mock battles staged for him. "He no coward!" Turkey would always exclaim to the flustered bird on its retreat after a contest. "He fool! No know when beat! He *Yank-ee* bird!"

"Yes," Grandfather would add, "a true Yankee bird, a stubborn bird of a true heart, whom shall always return even if beaten, and pursue his tormentors to face then again!"

The comments always drew a great laugh from both men in those days when it was proven white and Indian could live peacefully in Wyoming together, before forces from beyond their control forced a wedge between them which still lasts to this very day. Never once in those days did I notice any angst between the normal settlers and the Indians, Paxtang boys excluded, for every Indian knew to stay clear of Hanover Township, nor did I see a hatful word or look pass between white or Indian. Traders such as Hollenback always welcomed them with a hearty handshake and pat on the back. I myself remember Colonel Denison holding Queen Ester once, not letting her on her way when she came to trade at Hollenback's store until she heartily promised to bring more Indians to trade with them on her next visit. Such were the days when the world turned on a more peaceful and sensible axis, days now lost forever, unfortunately.

I sat this day on the front porch, for I had arisen early. The visions of the dreaded pest-house haunted me so. I watched Coward peck at the ground with his hens, all content and peaceful in the early light of dawn, oblivious of the past, or the future, only interested in the day at hand, the here and now. He reminded me of most Indians I had known, if not for their feathers, but for their manner of life. Coward was strange in other ways, too, for he had seemed to ally himself with Queeny, our dog. Queeny's coop being near the hen house, under the sweeping and shielding branches of a pine tree, many I morning I would find Coward roosting on a branch just over the coop, with Queeny all rolled over on her back just below him. Both seemed the best of friends. Many other days it was not uncommon to see Queeny lying on the cool grass in the summer looking lazily at Coward pecking away just in front of her, and I swear her eyes bore a look of contentment. Thus Coward had made himself a strong ally to protect his roost from the many opossums, raccoons, weasels, and foxes plaguing the other henhouses of Wyoming. Had not the Indians done the same allying themselves to the British bulldog? Another thing, if you left Coward be and did not provoke him, you could live beside him in peace all of your born days. But when you pushed, or confronted him, or threatened his flock, all hell would be to pay. Perhaps there is a certain lessen in that old tough bird of long ago.

Anyways, I always liked this time of the morning, just before the dawn, before the light of day shone on the noon marks on the cabin door, regulating time and allowing so much time to do this or that task. I liked its peaceful and unfettered air and would sometimes just watch the fog form, roll, and lift through the valley below, with each new gust of wind revealing a new section of the valley from its whiteness, as if being born anew to the day from it. Wyoming was so beautiful. In such moments I had little doubt why everyone held their right to it with such a fanatical resolve. It is from such people overcoming great odds that great nations are born. For if such people did not exist, in the end the nation would not exist.

"Get you some mush and milk," a voice suddenly jolted me out of my trance-like illusion. "You hear boy?"

I turned and looked up at Grandpa through soulful eyes. I must have, for he softened and sat besides me on the porch, following my eyes to the beautiful valley spreading out before us. "It is a fine place," he said with a sigh. "That is why your Pa is out fightin' for it against the cussed British."

"But what about the Injuns here abouts?" I asked.

"That, my boy, is question bothering most folks here abouts now," Grandpa said. "Ya see yer Pa and the rest of them signed up to defend the valley proper, and was only called out of the valley when things was looking pretty bad for General Washington's army, and now that things is lookin' a bit sour in these parts, most folks thinks they should be called back to the valley. Denison himself has sent a letter off lately to our Roger Sherman." He paused for a moment and turned towards me. "Ya know who Roger Sherman is, don't ya boy? He's what they calls our representative in the Continental Congress, well anyways, he sent a letter from us all asking our rightful troops be sent back to defend the home they was a supposed to be defending in the first place. Hopefully they'll listen, then your Pa and the others shall be back directly."

I nodded, though I remember thinking at the time it to be strange, for just a fortnight ago we saw off with hooting and hollering some thirty men under Captain Strong and Jameson, and how Obadiah Gore had recently visited recruiting for the greater army. And as I recall Captain Durkee himself made a long agonizing ride in the dead of winter to offer his troops to General Washington. It made no sense to me, but I left it alone as a matter for the grown ups, for I had greater troubles at the moment which I promptly addressed.

"Does it hurt, Grandpa, to take on the sickness to stop it?" I asked. This, too, made little sense to me and I remember the stark fear it sent running down my spine me clear to this day.

"Don't fret son," Grandpa said. "If'n it brought any danger to you do ya think your ma would agree to it? Or me self for that matter?"

"No, I reckon not," I said.

"It's the best way we know how to prevent the *pox*. After you and your brother gets a piece of the scab you'll be safe from it all your live-long days. It's a good thing, son." Grandpa turned towards the bustling noises in the cabin behind us. "Well everybody's up now, you fetch your bowl and eat, boy, while I get the cart hitched up to Old Mose."

The fact that he named his horse after my father, or perhaps me, is something I regret never asking my Grandpa about, but I sensed it was about something back in Connecticut, if not mere happenstance. Some things it's just not proper for a young one to ask about, for I do remember the motto of those days, children should be seen and not heard, was taken quite literally. I remember it odd at the time of my family to allow me and my younger brother to sit proper at the table-board, for it was the custom of the day that only adults sat proper at the table, and the children waited out in the wings, fed after the adults had their fill. How times have changed, but most folks thought nothing of such practices, it was just the way it was, is all. Besides, though most people do not know it, it was the custom of the Indians to not even name their children until they had seen at least five summers of age in those times, that being the cut-off which they figured if they had survived that long they had a greater chance to see further days. What with cholera, the measles, mumps, and deadly small pox, for the Indians, though they loved their children deeply and did spare the rod on them, much unlike their white counterparts, a name drew an attachment to a memory which was better well forgotten, for its was not uncommon for only one out of three children to survive past five. Such were the times, and different people responded in different ways, is all.

After our quick breakfast Mother had us disrobe and put our proper clothes in a bundle, and dressed us in awful raw linen nightshirts, nothing more than crudely fashioned sheets of rough linen with holes simply cut in their top for our heads, with a hemp cord tied about our waists to hold them fast. She explained the examining committee had strict orders for all visiting the pest-houses in regard to a change of clothes to prevent the spread of the horrid disease. Oh, I often wonder if the present generation have but a faint idea of just how much this deadly plague was dreaded?

Ma then ushered I and Will to the two wheeled cart to which my Grandfather had hitched Old Mose. I, my mother, and Will climbed into the back of it while Grandfather walked along side of the cart guiding Old Mose along with a long stick. Some folks used a whip, especially with oxen, which some people, one of them being Sebastian Strope from up on the Wysox Creek, grew very agile with. It was said he could snap the head off a rattlesnake at some twenty feet, he was so proficient. But Grandpa didn't take to such things, preferring his stick and his harsh tongue to provide all the discipline he needed for Old Mose. People nowadays accustomed to riding in the wagon proper would have had a rude awakening back in those days. Most folks walked, the roads being no more than slightly widened footpaths. The room in wagons, especially the great Conestoga wagons of the day, were designed to move freight alone, for it was such a trial to get the wagons through the tight trails and over swollen rivers, that every inch in them was for freight, not people. The Indians in these parts mostly walked as well, the woods were not accommodating for horses, with little grazing except the plentiful wild grape vines, oh, how the whole area was covered with them. The only other thing were sparse saplings under the trees. After slaying one Indian in battle, the soldiers found no less than thirteen pairs of moccasins in his pack, attesting to just how far they walked. Before the days the war drove that eternal wedge between us and the Indians many would stop at Wyoming, as it lay on the Great Warrior Trail stretching from the Great Head at Onondaga about the finger lakes to points far south. As it was the custom of the day all homes on the frontier were open to traveling guests, Indian and white, believe it or not. If one had a window one would place a German candle in it as it was called, a beacon for the traveler to know a warm heart and hearth waited him. Well, I recall one time an Indian telling my Grandfather he walked from the great council fire at Onondaga all the way to the Choctaw and Creek nations in what is now Alabama country, and was returning with the answer to the question the Great Head at Onondaga presented them. Latter on, when one of the Harvey's was captured, he was taken to Niagara and adopted into a Indian party which went to the far lands beyond Lake Superior hunting, trapping and spreading the great Iroquois culture. They got around great for only walking. The Iroquois of the time were truly remarkable.

As for grasslands upriver, once you got above Wyoming there was nothing but solid forest all the way to Ontario, with the exception of the Genesee Valley, and little spots around abandoned Indian villages. Small fields and such, mostly grown up with wild rye or that tough no-good-for-nothing-but-to-make-a-broom Indian grass. There was a spot above Wyalusing called Misicum, which was very popular among folks farming up in those parts, and they would canoe or pole their rafts for miles to collect its grass, good English grass someone had cultivated so long ago the Indians even forgot whom, exactly. From there it was up to Sheshequin for the next grass, over seven feet tall in the summer, but was the worthless Indian grass. As the modern settler looks around I often wonder if he knows of the struggles to tame every inch of the land he now takes for granted, and looking out in the wide fields dotting the mountains and vales, does he even consider it once to be a solid forest? And that the grass had been all brought in and planted after a painful rooting up of the great, ancient, and towering trees, left alone since God himself planted them, to attest to their height, for the Indians had no axes to fell them. A monumental task indeed, seeing the thought of the day was to start a farm where the great trees towered on the hilltops because they grew where the ground was the most fertile. It was not until latter they figured out the fertility of the river flats caused by flooding. Flooding was a nuisance to be avoided in those hard times. So when they set up their *pitch,* or claim to the soil, they had to fell the greatest of the trees. Such times, such men, we owe more than we can ever truly imagine to those whom literally conquered the ground, as well as the nation. If we possess but one percent of their grit and determination we will be the greatest nation on the earth. Forgive my rambling, but I can still see these men long departed, tall, towering John Franklin, sure and brave Zebulon Butler, resolute John Jenkins, and I wish only to try and convey their great spirit and resolve, for it is unmatched to this day, and to awaken it again in the American heart is my fondest wish. What they suffered through and did was unbelievable and truly remarkable, in my estimation, at least.

> *Such men will shine*
> *In the annals of time*
> *When the lives they had to live*
> *Demanded all they could give*
> *For the hope of their children led them along*
> *So children don't say, how they lived was wrong*
> *For they lived every day with you on their mind*
> *So in passing memory, do not leave them behind*
> *And in honoring their memory you shall*
> *Let them know forever, they did not fail*
> *To their honor, hope, and memory be true*
> *For their hope is still here, and it is you*

And in the peaceful morning of this day my Grandfather led us silently along the trail to the dreaded pest-house. We passed many roving patrols of militia scouts, each stopping to ask just what we were about, nodding upon hearing the inoculation explanation, followed always by the question from Grandfather on how the new forts that had been ordered built were coming along; especially Fort Jenkins, ordered to be built near the fort the suspected Tories, the Wintermoots, up near Exeter. All patriots in the valley would rest better when Fort Jenkins was complete; one built by men whose patriotism was beyond reproach-the Jenkins. Besides, the explanation the Wintermoots told everyone questioning them of just why they had built their fort rang hollow in the ears of the patriots. They built it to protect the valley against wild Indians, they said, only sneering when asked of the Tory menace.

Upon finally reaching the pest-house, we did not have to be told we had arrived by the horses and carts sitting patiently rods away and upwind from the tainted cabin. A lone sour-eyed sentry sat, not stood, twenty feet in front of the pest-house door, openly disgruntled of just how he drew such duty, and not happy at all with the response. So he had reached a compromise, he would sit far from the door and watch, for if any fool stumbled into it, it would be his own fault, for he would not leave for a fortnight until the doctor, or matron of the pest-house, an unfortunate mid-wife or such, gave him a clean bill of health. Only the children were allowed to leave once inoculated, knowing their care to be too much for the overtaxed matrons, trusting their parents to keep them within the dooryard of the cabin with a clear warning posted for anyone passing by to see.

So with a scooting hand from our mother, whom advanced only as far as the disgruntled sentry, I and Will trudged with bowed heads to the awaiting door of dread.

Such misery I had not witnessed before in my short life, for the battle was yet to come, but in sheer misery this pest-house had few rivals. Men, women, and some children, from whom I adverted my shocked eyes as to not draw their curse to me through knowing them, lay strewn on a hasty bed of misery, covered with festering scabs and all bearing a look beseeching all, and God himself, for pity. And the sickly smell of stale breath, bodily functions soiling beds, puss, and such, made my stomach heave. I found my hands clutching my younger brother, if not to reassure him as to comfort myself. A lone man, the bags under his eyes attesting to his many hours in the miserable house, rose from one of the beds and waved us to him with a tired hand. I recognized him, Doctor Gustin. A few other pot-marked faced women, the sign that they had survived the disease in former times and thus had immunity to it, hovered about the beds, giving water and what comfort they could to the suffering souls. But one old woman, sitting by a bedside slowly sewing a bag closed over a prostrate soul with coins over his eyes, drew the most horror from I and my brother. So much so we froze with fear upon nearing the bed, neither us willing to take one more step forward, but rather backwards, towards the door.

Doctor Gustin, marching forward and taking us by the scruff of our necks, persuaded us otherwise. He stopped us in a far corner where a man lying covered with boils looked soulfully up to us.

The doctor took a small instrument and went at I and Will's exposed upper arms, making a slight cut in them. He then turned by light of a pine knot jammed in the chinking of the cabin over the poor soul's head, and played at one of his festering boils, noticeably adverting his gaze from the man's pitiful eyes. "This will be the last this day," I heard him whisper to the doomed man before turning with his ill-gotten treasure on the end if his instrument towards I and Will. He went to my cut first, carefully coating it with the puss under my terrified eyes. Releasing my shaking arm he turned to Will, whose hand I clasp all the more tightly as he endured the procedure with tears and the most pitiful and pleading look in his eyes, beseeching his older brother to come to his rescue and save him from the doctor of death in his horrid place. But all I could do was to bear the suffering as he, and with a nod towards the door from Doctor Gustin we both sprinted to it, never more glad to breath unfettered and clean air as that day, bursting through that door of the horrid pest-house.

We sprinted into God's clear air towards our mother, pacing nervously about the sentry, until his sudden rise from the ground and shining bayonet stopped us dead in our tracks.

We looked up to mother, feeling doomed and betrayed. She looked to the sentry. He sighed and rolled an eye to the bundle of clothes she held.

"Over there lads," he ordered, "by the sheets hanging about the branches on the far trees yonder. Disrobe, put your clothes on the fire, and then dress back into your proper clothes!" With that he motioned for our mother to toss us the bundle and sat back down, his face clearly showing his disgust for this most disagreeable service.

We needed no more coaxing. If that is all that need be done to rid of us of this most horrid place, we willfully complied. We scampered over to the sheets, threw down the bundle, and ripping off our pest clothes, and placed them on the fire at the direction of the lone man with a mask covering his lower face and an extremely long stick. He gestured with the stick to toss our pest clothes onto a certain spot on the blazing fire. We carefully placed them just so, and with a nod from him, turned back to our bundle. Pulling our clothes from it, we hastily dressed as we ran to our awaiting mother. With a slow nod from the disgruntled sentry, she ushered us up the bank to our awaiting Grandfather and cart.

Grandfather, noticing our rush, pulled the pipe from his mouth as if to ask us where the devil chased us from, but stayed silent instead, finding the answer in a quick change of wind caring the stench of the pest-house upon it. His feet moved all the faster from the smell. Turning Old Mose about, he trotted as fast as his and Old Moses' legs could manage, ignoring waves from the others gathering about to take their turn at inoculation. I suddenly felt an awful pity for the donor man, wondering if Doctor Gustin told the man each time he lanced one of his festering boils this would be the last out of pity for the man, or he truly hoped it would be the last. A doctor in those days needed a special grit few possess today.

Chapter Four

Well after the *pox* had passed and the last of the forts neared completion, a certain calm once again descended over Wyoming. Though often, to this very day, the sight of the poor forsaken donor man still haunts my soul well into to my old age. I can still see him in my nightmares with his long, damp, and dirty flaxen hair spreading across a filthy pillow, soiled with the puss of many a boil, which showed against his ash-colored skin. And those pleading eyes, reaching out and searching humanity for aid from his suffering, with none knowing how to give it, but with a prayer and a swallow of rum. Oh, how empty their gestures seemed! Oh, the *pox,* the bane of all mankind!

This day sitting on the porch I heard a ruckus coming up from the south. Queeny's ears perked up long afore I actually caught sight of the culprits, but I knew whom it must be the moment I saw the dogs running to and fro up the trail, circling around a tall man in saddle, singing at the top of his lungs one of those flowing songs of yesteryear. Though that wide-brimmed black slouch hat he always sported cover his bowed head, I knew him in an instant. Captain Franklin, who had made his pitch down Huntington and Salem way. Seeing the dogs, I knew he had come up here on one of his hunts, and being so late in the day, I knew it must be a coon hunt.

Watching Will dart out of the cabin door, I watched his eyes glow in anticipation, as mine, for Captain Franklin had taken a shine to us boys and felt it his personal duty, being Pa's friend and all, to see in on us boys and Ma every once in a while. We did so enjoy our outings with him.

We watched him slowly ride up, his head bowed under that wide brim, whistling and singing to his heart's content, and waited 'til he stopped his horse near the hitching post in front of the porch. His head slowly rose from under that wide brim with his piercing blue eyes glaring right at us, with a great smile stretching ear to ear. "Boys," he said with a nod.

We stood in great anticipation, hanging on his next

words. The lumps in our throats forbade us to speak.

He looked down at his dogs and Queeny openly running to and fro about them. "Dogs was getting mighty antsy. Been a while since they been out, so you think you boys is up to coming on a coon hunt?" Captain Franklin asked.

We burst at the words. Dancing and smiling, we said, "We sure is, Uncle John!" before running up to his horse and greeting all his dogs, which licked our faces and whined, seeming as anxious as we for the outing.

"Where's your Ma and your Grandpa?" Uncle John asked, watching our eyes glaring at his long rifle. I always marveled at the long barrels of the day and how those tough frontiersmen handled them in the thick sugarbush and tight trails and such. Just loading the things was a devil in the first place, having to literally hammer the ball down the spiraling in the barrel. The ramrods alone stood well over my height alone, but the thought of the time was because the powder of the day being poorer, the longer the barrel, the more of it would burn before reaching the end of the barrel, thus greatly reducing the fouling and giving the added advantage of more accuracy and greater range. As days went on and better powder was developed the barrels got shorter. But in those days, the longer the better.

"Why big Johnny Franklin!" a voice suddenly yelled from the door. "What brings you this way?"

"Just a visit, Isaac," Franklin said, lifting his rifle and swinging a leg over the saddle. He promptly slid from the saddle and stood tall with his four dogs swarming about his feet. "Roger Sherman, John Durkee, General Washington, and Zeb!" he said down to the dogs with a pat to each of their heads. "You get on and play about with Queeny, sun's still a bit high to head out on the hunt just yet!" The dogs yelped and scattered about as if understanding his words. But the word hunt drew the most attention from I and Will. We beamed up at Grandpa in anticipation and scampered to the porch away from the roving dogs underfoot.

"A hunt, huh?" Grandpa asked, walking out the door and looking down at us wide-eyed boys. He waved Johnny up to the porch and sat down in his rocker, rubbing his chin.

"Yep," Franklin answered, easing his rifle, his 'peacemaker', as he called it, along the wall. He sat on the stoop. "Figured the boys was a getting as antsy as the dogs, and figured it about time to give them both a run."

Grandpa rolled a sly eye towards us and finally let a smile break through his grim look. "I reckon that'd be fine fer the boys, but my old bones just ain't up to it," he said with a nod to us boys.

Why, I and Will nearly jumped clear to the moon, as I recall. We looked forward to such outings so in those simple days now long past. We both knew what was next without asking and looked to Johnny. He smiled and waved his wide-brimmed hat towards the road after giving grandpa a wink.

"Yes," he said, "you best fetch old Quocko if'n he's about, seeing how's yer grandpa ain't feeling up to a hunt."

We both scurried up the road for the Martin's cabin to fetch their man Quocko, whom I do think enjoyed our little outings as much as I and Will. It just wouldn't be the same without him, the dear soul. We stopped long enough to look back over our shoulder to Johnny who instantly said, "Call them along," for he knew we wished to have the dogs accompany us.

"Roger Sherman!" we called to the eldest of the pack, whom dutifully answered and ran to us. In another second we was up the road, singing and whooping with joy, with the oddly named dogs howling all around us. What a sight we must have been and old Quocko must've heard us coming a mile away, for he always met us halfway up the road from our place, every time. We'd always meet him and he'd be wearin' a smile that would put anyone else's to shame. Seeing those grinning teeth a stretchin' across that old dark face still does my heart good if only to reflect on it after all these forlorn years. I like to remember old Johnny and Quocko just as they was, though Johnny's well into old age now. Dear Quocko's just a dear memory of those simple times, which were forever changed by that horrible battle he fell in, defending hearth and kin. Oh, what a horrible price is paid in war, for it only seems to take the best. The best of times as well as men.

I reckon a word about them odd names Johnny named his coon dogs should be said, for I admit most folks about then thought it odd, too. You see Johnny was one who had what folks would call an odd sense of humor, and like most in the time took the happenings that were changing everything to heart, and it reflected in all they did, for folks could sense the great changes rolling through those times, somehow everyone knew. Some ignored it, while others resisted it, and some wholeheartedly embraced it, which was most about Wyoming then, I durst say. Well in that, Johnny named his prized coon dogs. Roger Sherman, for our representative in Congress, whom I might add has the distinction of being the only one to put his name to all the great documents of the age, and had a hand in the great Declaration, itself, thus Johnny Franklin named his best dog. John Durkee, whom had a great hand in laying out our original settlement and was quite a hero in the Pennamite Wars, who at the time was off fighting in the war. General Washington, whose fame proceeds him, even in that day, and last of all just plain old Zeb, who most folks said was named after our own Colonel Zebulon Butler, who himself did not take a liking to having a coon dog named for him, but most folks knew it just the same, thus just the name Zeb. Latter on Johnny said he had a mind to name one Ben Franklin, another man whom held great respect from all, but thus the cruel hand of war stripped him of that hope.

Looking back, I do not wonder why folks that ain't been through hell, seem to have such a hard time getting a true understanding of it. For if anyone was to tell us all that the many buildings, farms, stores, and such, would have been totally destroyed in them days, we would have thought him soft in the head for sure, a bit crack, I think was the term bandied about them, which would latter just become, 'cracked.' And the many faces I still do mourn, including those dogs we spent such joyous times with in our youth. They too would not survive the battle. We lost all but the clothes on our backs. I wonder if any soul reading this in reflection can look about him or her to their own pet, desk, chair, and picture of a dear loved one a hanging on the wall, and imagine them all ravaged, burned, and destroyed; everything. Look out the window to the street and to the other houses and think yourself secure, as we did, and then imagine it all gone in one day! Such was our devastation, not only of our homes, but of our hearts! I tell you what a terrible price was paid, for old John Bull sitting in far away England did not seem so far away then, and he being the most powerful nation in the world at the time, I tell you his wrath was as strong as his resolve! What a war! What a poor skinny little boy taking on the strongest man in the world! That was us taking on John Bull and his like! But what is so amazing, we won! But I tell you that lad that was America was beaten, broken, and ravaged in more ways than one before he finally rose free in the end. That should never be forgotten, and if you walk these hills and look out to these strong mountains, I hope you full well understand the price paid for it, for it was most steep. Men like old Quocko, never knowing the liberty we talked about, but willingly laying down his life for it; or for its simple hope, in the end. He laid it down not for himself, but for me, you, and all those to come, so God bless Quocko Martin and all the tired bones of his comrades still lying on that field. Walk it lightly when you do, for beneath it beats the heart of a nation.

Chapter Five

Just afore dusk we set out, for we had to make camp far upriver. Johnny said the best coon lay up there, and the closer we could get to any old Indian village the better, he said, for they had the peculiar habit of a leavin' the critters near their village alone in summer so as to have them near in the winter. Right smart I might say, but I never knew a white man to take much stock in Indian ways. To them you kill the easiest and nearest game you can, and never seem to worry on the morrow. In these things I think we could learn something from the Indians, but it is not our way, and we can be rather stubborn. It's almost to say our ways are best, and damn everything else. But after necessity makes our pride fade, we do learn of other people's ways, but we never admit it. Thus the wisdom of the good book; be humble in all that you do.

We set upon the mouth of a creek on the river and went to making our camp with the dogs getting more restless the darker it got. Tethered and tied, all but Queeny, that is, they pulled and tugged at their ropes, but dared not howl for fear of Johnny. They knew when the time was right, so they waited. I and Will being just as antsy we understood, for the thrill of the hunt is something. We went about fetching wood and taking care of the horses while Johnny and Quocko attended to the other matters of the hunt.

How we would scrabble to set up the camp, then wait and look with anxious eyes from the fireside, waiting for Johnny to cock an eye to the Quocko, grab up his sacks and pistols, and finally let the dogs loose. Then it was an all out run into the woods and through the abandoned round Indian fields dotting the banks, all on the trail of the fat coons rising to roam the night. We'd walk along, anxious to hear that first howl and hollow bark of Roger Sherman. Then the hunt was on, we'd scramble on through the night, our blood racing when that howl turned longer, announcing the dogs had treed a coon.

Well this night, we come upon one after another, with Johnny and Quocko dispatching one treed coon after another, with I and Will fetching them afore the dogs could tear them up. We'd shoo them on and they be off on a new sent, a howling and carrying on something fierce. Big, fat, coon, filled our sacks in no time, and we had to stop to sit some down at some marked place afore going on to the next place.

Pretty soon Johnny waved Quocko on while he took care of a particularly big coon, one of them ones benefiting from the Indian way of things, no doubt. I and Will ran along with Quocko to the next tree, with Queeny, though not a coon dog, barking and carrying on something fierce. Now in them days we did have dogs to run deer, wolves, and such, but we also had the bear dogs, and if Queeny was anything, she was a bear dog. That's when we all started a lookin' to the dark forest with a different eye, even the coon dogs.

Quocko yelled for us to help him shoo around a big coon the dogs had treed in a small tree just over his head. Its eyes shone in the moonlight atop that tree a swaying back and forth from the weight of that fat coon. He fired one pistol, then the next, but missed that swaying coon. The closer it crept down to the ground from that swaying tree, the more Quocko swore at it, fumbling to reload his brace of pistols afore that coon just scampered away, for the creek lay just a rod away.

"Them dogs will a tear it up fer sure!" he yelled to us. "And if'n it gets them in the water it'll drown them fool dogs, fer sure it will, then Capt'n John will have himself a right smart fit he will!"

Between him yellin' and them dogs a yipping and howling something fierce, we turned our back to Queeny's warning, though she stood firm with the hair of her whole back standing straight and snarling something fierce. We stumbled to the tree swinging long sticks up at that fat coon a swaying back and forth. Quocko stood swearing at that coon and cracking away, missing every time.

Then all the word seemed to explode with a glittering black bear bursting through it all, snarling, swatting at the dogs, and growling as I never heard anything a growl afore. I and Will spun about, scampering up the nearest tree ourselves, feeling much like a coon.

The dogs yipped and nipped at that beast, Queeny a chomping at its rear legs as a good bear dog would, and snarling and barking. Quocko scampered up the nearest tree by him and swore up a storm so fierce at that big black bear I swear it make my hair curl. His pistols did crack one after another between his oaths, but not fast enough to suit I and Will in our tree. Losing all fear of heights we climbed as fast as any old coon until the branches started snapping at the top of that old hemlock. The loud report of Johnny's old 'peacemaker' never seemed so welcome to us.

All fell silent after the loud report but a few whimpering dogs. We stared down from the boughs of that hemlock and dared not even breath when a hearty laugh sent a shock through our bones.

"You best get down from there, Quocko, afore you break that twig you're a resting on snaps!" Johnny's voice boomed on the tail end of the laugh.

I and Will scampered down out of the tree in a heartbeat, there to see bug-eyed Johnny Franklin standing with one foot atop that midnight black bear, his grin a shinning as bright as the moon above.

"Boys," he said with a nod, "glad to see you fine and well." Queeny rambled up to us sporting a few fresh gashes glistening in the moonlight on her side. We fell and both heartily embraced her, our hero, and swore never to ignore her warning again. And we never did, God rest her soul.

A twig snapped and down came Quocko, tumbling and rolling right up next to the bear. He screamed and struggled to get away when big John's hand, I never seen a man with such big hands, reached down and lifted him up and away from the great beast.

"Sakes alive, Capt'n," Quocko gasped, backing away and shaking his head. "That there is one big bear!"

Another snap of a branch sent that fat coon tumbling

down to the ground and scampering away in the night, with no one, even a smarting Roger Sherman, giving it chase.

"Best let him be," Johnny said, watching him go. "We got something better on this coon hunt." He bent down and ran his hand through that glistening black coat in the moonlight. "It'll make a right fine coat," he said, more to himself than anyone else. "And meat for all for weeks to come, I durst say!" Taking out his long knife he immediately got to a gutting and skinning that great beast which must have well weighed close to nine hundred pounds, if not more.

So we made camp right then and there with us boys and a shaken Quocko going back to fetch up our things from our first camp. Johnny Franklin sat right there and busied himself with a skinning his prize. Quocko put flint to steel to start a right smart fire before we left. A good thing, for Johnny wasn't a stopping for nothing, and the fire would shine as a beckon for us in the dark forest. No one seemed to pay the Injun and Tory threat much mind, for we had conquered a greater beast and everything seemed to pale in light of it. A whimpering Roger Sherman and company rolled up near the fire and waited with Johnny, a smarting from their wounds so much it took the hunt out of them, and that's quite something for coon dogs I might say.

When we fetched back all the camp things, we returned to see Johnny sitting by the fire cutting at some meat with that long knife of his. When the Indians called the white frontiersmen Long Knifes, they wasn't a kidding none, for I tell you that knife of Johnny's stretched a full cubic if nothing less. And them long rifles, I still marvel on how they trudged through the thick sugarbush with the long things. They were something, all of them.

Johnny looked up from the flames glistening in his bright blue eyes and raised one of his bloody hands to wave. "We'll be eating fine tonight," he said with a grin. "Bear's a bit stringy, but it's a fine meal, puts me in mind of dog, it does, maybe they's cousins in times past."

"I reckon so," Quocko said, "I thought the same before, I has at that." He sat down near the fire and groaned, putting a hand to his backside. "His meat will go a long ways as relieve the suffering he caused my backside, yes, it will."

Johnny grinned and winked to us boys. He always took a shine to a sparking a fire in Quocko by some quaint remark. This time would be no different than any other, so he rolled his eyes to Quocko and rubbed his chin, leaving a bit of blood on it, but that never seemed to bother the likes of Johnny. Blood, dirt, and sweat, they seemed to be made of it, and if either of them was took away, I think they would have fell apart.

"Old Dan Walter," he said looking down at the meat sizzling on some hot stones. "Friend of yours, ain't he, Quocko, being a man of color like you and all?"

"Quocko groaned and stretched out on the ground. "Reckon so," he said. "But what's that got to do with things?"

Franklin laughed and turned an eye to us boys. "You know of him don't you boys?" he asked.

We both nodded and gathered around the whimpering dogs, checking their wounds and such.

"Was caught by the Injuns wasn't he, Johnny?" I said.

"That he was," Johnny said. "That he was." He let his grin grow again and turned back towards Quocko.

Quocko just shook his head at him.

"But that ain't the end of it boys," Johnny said. "You see when they took him they adopted him right smart and fine and one of their finest squaws, an Indian princess, and a fine figure for an Indian, or any woman, she was, took a shine to him." He chuckled for a moment before continuing. "Well they took old Dan and a dressed him up fine all Indian like, smothered his skin with bear grease, and painted him up fine, they did. He went along a grinning and a smiling until they led him to the fine princess and announced he was to marry her. Well old Dan took a fit and denounced her right then and there in front of her people and all." Johnny shook his head. "Not

39

the smartest thing to do, boys, not at all!" He shook his head at Quocko, whom only scowled back at him as if to ask what has any of this to do with him?

"Well boys they right then and there stripped him down, kicked and abused him in a most grievous manner, and finally made him run the gauntlet, they did, which he barely survived, and still bears the marks and lingering pains of it to this day," Franklin said, shaking his head. "But what is the strangest thing is to look at old Dan's wife now, the one he took after he escaped and returned to Wyoming."

"What of her?" Quocko reluctantly asked.

"You know her, don't ya boys?" Franklin asked us.

We both nodded, now drawn into the tale.

"Well then you know she's not much more than the plainest of ladies," Franklin said, lifting a piece of the sizzling meat to his mouth to taste it. He chewed it and then smiled. "Nothing like fresh, fine meat, roasted fresh," he said. "There's the lesson boys, wherever life puts you make the best of it! If you go a coon hunting and kill a big bear instead, make a fire and roast its meat, and stretch its hide to make you a warm coat against the cold winter! And if'n you get caught by the Indians and are given a princess, well take her for all she's worth, ain't no shame at all in it! The shame is a turning down a princess for a plain woman! You just ask old Dan Walter! Ain't that right Quocko!"

Quocko tried to hold back a smile, but the thought of his friend Dan probably now pondering on the same thing, brought a great smile to his face. "I reckon that's so," he said on a laugh. "Leastways that's what I knows old Dan would say if'n he was here, I know it to be true, I do!"

Both he and Johnny shared a hearty laugh that seemed to pass right over I and Will's heads.

But we laughed just the same, we did, there in those woods a feasting on fresh bear meat. Oh what memories of simpler times before more complicated days. What a time I and Will had that night. What a time.

Chapter Six

Summer came and went with its coon hunts, fishing, swimming, and such, but so the world turns with its seasons; its revolutions, its new turns. I will never forget in those days the messengers returning from Philadelphia and Hartford and the like, talking of the great men they witnessed there, each carrying something of an air, some of confusion, and others of a certain angst, but all carrying something of the new turn in the way of things for all of mankind. Oh such days, mysterious, uncertain, but great. I tell you the only way to catch the gist of it all was to live it, for there truly was something in the air. I hope something of it shall always remain, and never fade in the winds of change blowing through the eons.

Everyone would gather around the green, Hollenback's store, Forty Fort, or such a place, to hear the tales of those witnessing the great men of change first hand. It was one of them, I can't remember just whom exactly, for there are many lost to the ages, but this one told with swirling hands how one of the great men, a Virginian, a man of enlightenment, equated the times with a new instrument he had acquired from Europe, an Orrery, a strange device which had all the planets represented in small orbs on rods attached to gears, wires, levers, and cranks to a special table. The huge apparatus sat atop a Hepplewhite-style table, I believe they called it. Strange how I can remember such details and forget the man telling the sorry, but such is the way of things. Sometimes the message is greater than the messenger. Well anyways, when that certain enlightened gentlemen would turn a handle located on the special table all the planets would turn in orbit around the sun. Quite a fascinating device to say the least, which still boggles my mind after all these years, the way that forgotten patriot described it so fluently with his waving hands and marvelous words, his eyes alive with wonder. He would tell how the enlightened gentlemen would then tell his fellows as he turned the crank on the table that with each new turn, or revolution, the planets would change from night to day, and in the long run from spring to fall, and fall to winter, and then do it all over. A new turn gentlemen, he would say, or if you may have it, a *revolution*. Thus this enlightened gentlemen had justly termed what was happening to his country, a new turn, a revolution. What men, what times. Shall the world ever witness their like again?

Well as time went on other messengers came, none the more than Joel Phelps, a neighbor and man I do remember along with the grim message he bore coming by our cabin one fine fall day. I remember it well as the frost was late that year and had not set, which could be a good thing for folks or a bad thing, as the term *Indian Summer* was to come from just such late falls. Most folks pay no mind to it and remember it favorably for the lengthy warm weather, but the term then held a much more sinister meaning and brought nothing but dread to our hearts. For it originated in Wyoming to warn of the Indians setting out on more raids against us on the frontier before holing up for the winter. One more rampage through the frontier, burning, plundering, and scalping if need be. Yes sir, it held a much different meaning back in those days.

Well Joel Phelps rode up all silent one day, his eyes wide and his face pale, not long, I guess, after he had actually returned from the failed scout which caused us all some great concern. Though his eyes were wide they held a gaunt, foreboding look, as a man who's come to tell you the well's dry and their ain't no sign of rain or something of the like. Joel rode his horse right up to the front of our porch and stared with hollow eyes at Grandpa sitting all fine and comfortable in his chair. Us boys hovered around but kept our distance, for the old adage children are to be seen and not heard was alive and well in those days. So we hovered by the porch post and clung to it, trying to stay silent and out from underfoot.

Strangely, Joel sat there for the longest moment as if the words clumped up in his throat. Grandpa just looked back curiously and continued puffing on his pipe. After a few minutes he finally raised his hand to pull the pipe from his mouth to speak.

Joel watched his hand slowly rise and somehow broke through the clump of words and gasped "Johnny Jenkins's been taken to hell or Tioga!"

Well Grandpa stopped his hand in mid-air and stared blankly at him for the longest moment as if the well had truly gone dry. All the hope everyone had for peace but a while longer faded, and the dark storm clouds of war showed clear on the horizon. Those terrible, dark, foreboding clouds of war started looming and would block out the sun about Wyoming for many years to come.

Us boys, though young, knew just what the open act of aggression meant, too, and we both gasped and collapsed down around the post. Both Grandpa and Joel cast a haunting look to us, but neither spoke. I heard Ma and Grandma gasp back inside the cabin door.

"Ain't the worst of it," Joel continued, suddenly finding his voice. "Sam Gordon's been taken too. It was that rat Parshall Terry! He's turned cold hard traitor, he has! To all his kith and kin! That whole lot upriver is mostly Tory bastards they is! Secord, the Depues, Pawlings, and all of them! They're a stirring up the Injuns something fierce no doubt! Butler and Brant are in their glory and our scalps will be the ones they is after!"

"My God," Grandpa gasped. "Is the militia to be called up? Are we to march?"

"I don't know," Joel said. "Colonel Denison is a thinking hard on things, he is, though. Says we's got to play it safe as not to rile the Injuns, for he says Ester can only hold them back so much, what with Butler and Brant about and all."

"How is his parents, Squire and his dear wife?" Ma's voice asked from behind the door.

Joel looked to the door and doffed his tri-cornered hat. "Well they is taking it hard, as one could imagine," he said. "I'm just about spreading the word, for I was there, and seen the look of the devil in all them Tories' eyes. They took our mounts, traps, rifles, and even our shoes, afore sending us back downriver, the bastards!" The words seem to burn through his throat, dredging up the most foul memories. He bowed his head and shook it in shame. His hand holding his hat fell limp to his side.

"Now son, you needn't fret so," Grandpa said. "I'm sure you all did all you could, the rats probably got the drop on you all."

"That they did," Joel answered. "That they did. They knocked old Quocko Martin clear off his horse. I thought they killed him they hit him so hard as to make an example for us all if'n we tried anything."

We all perked up at the mention of Quocko.

"He's fine though, but his ribs is surely sore," Joel said. "He's a tough old bird. Just the sort we need for the troubles a coming downriver from Tioga!"

"That he is," Grandpa said with a nod. "Was any others hurt?"

"No, just our pride," Joel said, turning his mount away. "So you folks keep a smart eye out for things, and if'n you see any feathered heads a poking around let 'em have a shot of lead and ask questions latter, for I tell you, no matter what Colonel Denison says, we is to have a mess of trouble from them, for they are much too tight with John Bull and his like. In that the Hanover boys is right. They will be trouble before it's all said and done!"

We all watched poor crestfallen Joel ride away without a word. I heard Ma and Grandma shuffle away from the door and whisper dreadful things between them. Grandpa just put his pipe back in his mouth and took a long draw on it, his eyes watching through the smoke to the far horizon, a horizon now filled with fear and dread, never to be the same.

Yes, I reckon it was right then and there the gloom started to descend over Wyoming. All sensed it, but none spoke of it. All knew and liked the popular John Jenkins and knew him to be a strong man of little words, but strong actions. All our imaginations shuddered at his fate, be it at the torture post or in one of the hellish British prisons. All our hearts went out to his dear Bethiah Harris, whom loved him so and patiently waited for him to make his mark and marry her. But a strong man, with a strong sense of responsibility, held off until he made his proper fortune as to provide for her the right way. Somehow all that seemed to fade though, in the face on the threat of the Tories and Indians. Perhaps one should act on his emotions despite proper manners, it seemed, for in the end true emotions such as pure love are so rare they should be acted upon posthaste. For who knows what the morrow may bring? I am sure Bethiah now felt the same, and poor John, too. But we all feared it to be too late, for war gobbled up all the good things in life and darkened all the souls of its participants.

Oh, how we feared what was to come. We all looked

around with a different eye after John Jenkins was taken. To the East and South we looked to see the British army about Philadelphia and New York City, but felt certain General Washington and his troops would keep them in check. It was to the North and West the foreboding clouds of war loomed most threateningly. In the West nests of Injuns lay everywhere in the dark folds of the forest, striking and fading back into it without any sign of their passing but burned farms and the shadows of the inhabitants, either scalped corpses or captives feared never to be seen again.

But from the North came the greatest fear, for the greatest nest, Fort Niagara, lay there. From it the British and hated Tories lay in wait, gathering their forces and whispering their lies in the Injuns' ears, biding their time until the moment was ripe to strike. When, we did not know. How we did not know. Their strength we did not know. We only knew it harbored a nest of villains from the hated Mohawk Brant to the traitorous Butlers, all bearing a certain hatred for us true patriots of Wyoming. And among their numbers more and more neighbors and friends flocked, especially from upriver, telling them of our designs, strengths, and weaknesses.

Oh what a time and thinking on it still makes my skin tingle, though some many years have past. It is a hard fear, and I hope Americans shall never feel it again, but at the same time such fears keep the dull knife sharp and rust from its blade. America must always have a sharp blade for this I know from enduring one of the most fearful times. Words are fine, but fade in the true emotion of things, and it is from the emotions which all men act in the end. It is from emotion all war is waged. Let us never forget that, brethren, never. Let the American blade be sheathed in times of peace, but never let it become dull and rust from neglect, for freedom demands it be drawn in its own defense, unfortunately. And the sharpest blade cuts he deepest.

Chapter Seven

With the chilling news of Jenkins and Gordon's capture by the Indians and Tories the air turned equally cold. The cold winds blew from the North in more ways than one, I tell you. Colonel Denison felt them just as keenly, reacting cold and firm, but in a wise way. One must know what lays ahead before one can truly make a wise decision, so he dispatched Lieutenant Asa Stephens upriver with a party of nine men to see exactly what was what and to capture a couple of the Tories if possible.

Well he returned, with five disgruntled souls in tow, and word of nests of Tories above Tunkhannock Creek. The news chilled us all the more, but none more than Colonel Denison. He immediately put out a call for some one hundred brave men to march upriver and clean it out once and for all, all the way to Chemung Village above Tioga if need be. Lieutenant Colonel Dorrance, taking over as second in command of the regiment from a disgruntled Lazarus Stewart, was to lead the expedition. A fine man with a stand up to your work attitude in manners as well as dress. If fact none dressed finer than Colonel Dorrance I recollect. He always appeared smart and proper in his uniform, and equally as well in his civilian dress, which colors seemed most loud and bright by today's standards, but not in the days this brave patriot lived, God rest his eternal soul. I remember seeing him once in a the brightest blue coat I have ever seen to this day, but somehow he seemed regal and smart in it nonetheless. Thus the old maxim 'clothes make the man' found no better representation.

Grandfather, though aged and with a touch of the rheumatism, as he called it, set out to answer the call, much to Grandma's and Ma's grief. They watched him silently put together his bundle, his eyes firm and full of resolve, a look which would not tolerate any argument.

Ma and Grandma watched silent from the table, both with there hands to their mouths and fidgeting all about, their eyes trying to catch Grandpa's. But he would have none of it. Seeing him move towards the mantle over the hearth both woman responded. Reluctantly, but just as stubbornly as Grandpa, they shuffled between Grandpa and the mantle bearing his trusty old rifle.

He stopped, looked them both in the eye, and bit his lip. Grandma put a hand to his shoulder without a word. Using the silent language of the eyes which only two people joined in matrimony for decades share, she eased him back to the table and a chair. Ma followed and put her own hand to his shoulder. "I know father," she whispered to him. " I know how the call of duty weighs heavy upon a man's conscience, but we've already too many men answering the call and suffering who knows where at this very moment." She put a hand to her chin and turned her eyes away, bearing that far away look she always had when thinking of Pa's sufferings in the army. "Let the younger souls take care of this business, though your heart be full of spirit your old bones may not. We need you here, you know we do, and I for one hope it never comes down to be needin' old men to go off and fight younger men's battles. By God I do."

Grandpa nodded and looked away from his rifle. "I fear for the storm that's comin' is all," he said. " If we can nip it in the bud afore it all starts and gets out of hand, I fer one, and all for it. I rather fight them Tories up there than in my own yard is all."

"Oh, Isaac," Grandma gasped, rolling an eye to I and Will gawking and taking everything in, "don't be talking of such in front of the children."

"They best know," Grandpa said, "fer a right smart shot of fear ain't always a bad thing! Keep's folk's mind's sharp, as well as their wit! And we sorely are in need of both in these uncertain times, we is! It'll keep them boys from a wandering too far away from the cabin." He turned and looked sternly at both of us, and I tell you the chill his old eye gave us both stretches across the ages and I feel it clear to this day as when I heard it firsthand, "They's feathered heads about looking to lift yer hair, and don't you fer doubt none, neither of you! Keep your eyes smart for it, young ones! Keep your eyes smart for it!"

Just then the fire cracked and sparked, sending embers flying all over the hearth, giving us all, even Grandpa, a start. Just as quick a sharp rap came to the door, nearly making us all jump out of our skin. I and Will scampered and run headlong for the loft thinkin' the entire Six Nations come callin' for our hair. We both squirmed under our rope bed and pulled the covers down tight to shield us, wishing for all the world we had Grandpa's gun with us.

Breathlessly we waited, listening for the door to creep open, not even daring to breathe in anticipation. We listened in hope of hearing old Grandpa's rifle crack and slay all the miscreants and both bolted out from under the bed just as quickly as we had scampered under it when a familiar voice sounded in the air. The brusque tones of Will Martin echoed through the cabin, followed by the equally familiar tones of our good friend, Quocko.

We skirted to the edge of the loft and peered down at the stout and round-faced man plopping down in a chair opposite Grandpa. We watched his hard businessman-like eyes look up to us with a glint and wink before turning to look back at Grandpa. His pale blue eyes always bore a serious look but when he looked to children. They seemed too soften then, betraying a deep concern for his fellow man, something one cannot hide. That is why him owning Quocko always puzzled me, for he seemed the least likely man to ever engage in such a thing. But such were the times one must remember, and one cannot judge unless one truly lived then. His transaction with Colonel Butler for Quocko was all the talk in many a corner in the cabins of Wyoming. No one ever really knew the gist of the transaction. Some thought it was for debt, and others just thought Martin, being a good business man, simply couldn't turn down a good bargain when offered one. But the meaning is lost with time, and with all the people involved now passed on, we may never know. But it is to say William Martin owned

Quocko on paper only, and there was no man freer about Wyoming than he. If fact, he embarked on many a scout before the battle on his own, defending his home, with no need to seek or ask permission of Will Martin. As I said before, Quocko Martin was of the best whom ever lived in Wyoming and I am proud to say I knew him.

So I and Will sat in the loft of that smoky cabin listening to every word Will and Quocko said. I tell you the smoke from the fires of passion burning in those days still stings my eyes to this day, drawing great tears, both good and bad. Will Martin and Quocko, as all men in those days about Wyoming, glowed with the fires of those passions. After affirming their mutual faith in the cause and cordially acknowledging Grandma and Ma, they said they stopped by because they knew Grandpa would be all a fire about a headin' out on the expedition and they came to reassure him all the best men would be on it and of the need for some good men to stay about Wyoming and watch the 'back door' while they was away a collecting up Tories. No telling what them Injuns would do despite Colonel Denison's great trust and faith in Queen Ester to contain all of the anxious Indians about Tioga Point. They, as well as many others about Wyoming, did not share his faith. To some an Indian like a panther, and a panther didn't settle down just because you feed him regular and pampered him. He'll strike when it's least expected, it is just his way, just like an Injun. You can't tame a truly wild beast no matter how hard you try. It's just the way of it, they argued.

Grandpa always scratched his head at such words and kind of shook his head, he being one whom always wanted to see the best in things, and everyone. But sitting in that loft after having the breeches a scared off from us, I and Will had to agree with the latter, for love of our hair. One could not risk such a thing on a mere hope. A panther was a panther, in a cage, or not.

But Grandpa had to agree the Tories must be dealt with, for with their resources from Niagara and with their silver tongues riling up the Injuns, they did pose a most awful threat to us about Wyoming. That was their nature. He had seen it and had no more love for the Tories than Lazarus Stewart and the Paxtang Boys had for the Indians, their creed being the only good Indian was a dead one. It is fair to say Grandpa, as well as Johnny Franklin, felt the same about the Tories to their dying days as did many an old patriot did about Wyoming. I know it to be true, God rest their souls.

So with Grandpa's blessing Will and Quocko Martin departed, full of purpose and each bearing that hard look of purpose in their eyes. From that day on I recollect I noticed that look every day in everyone's eyes until well after the war ended. As I said, some even carried it to the grave. Oh what a time to inspire such true, everlasting, and hard emotions in men. Every man of age carried it. Every soul breathed and fed on it. It carried them through their great sufferings, letting them emerge victorious in the end. Such a spirit is no brighter in men than when it is first born. This new spirit. This American spirit!

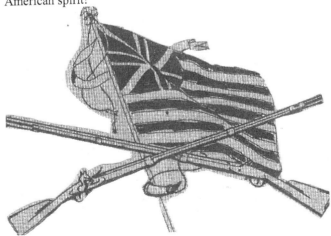

Chapter Eight

They marched right past our cabin on the day they returned, each man jack of the column beaming with pride and prodding on the crestfallen Tories in their charge, each tied together by a long rope looped over the necks of each one in line. Johnny Franklin's eyes never beamed more bright, I swear, him a sitting tall atop his great black mare, hollering and announcing to all they cleared the whole river of Tories. He took off his great wide-brimmed hat and waved it in the air when he saw I and Will, causing us to yell right along with him. We both smiled at the thick black collar on his new coat, our minds flashing back to the great coon hunt.

Quocko, riding just to his side, joined us, whooping and hollering. Standing up tall in the saddle he also waved his hat. Will Martin rode to the other side of the single file of tied Tories, his smart eye glaring down on them.

The sight of them did all our hearts good, for we all felt we had caged the wild panthers. The Simsbury Mines, a horrible prison in Connecticut, awaited them. From there they would cause us no harm. In there they would rot and we all felt fine and right about it, thinking of poor Johnny Jenkins rotting away in a hole at Fort Niagara and all.

At the head of the column rode Colonel Dorrance, sitting tall and stern, his eyes straight ahead, and grim face betraying no emotion. Even his old blanket coat looked good on him somehow, he just had that way about him. He did occasionally nod at the crowds a gathering around and cheering his triumphant column of men marching to Forty Fort to deliver their catch of some thirty hard and mean Tories to Colonel Denison. Many, including me, Will, and Grandpa, followed along the column all the way to Forty Fort, very relieved and happy.

That is why when just a few weeks later all our cheer faded upon word that the Tory Secord had petitioned the Continental Congress over the head of our Governor Trumbull, and had secured his and his fellow Tory's release on faulty pretenses. It came as quite a shock as most knew and thought we had proved that Secord, in the least, assisted escaping British soldiers to Sheshequin and then on to Niagara. How the fortunes of war do spin sometimes. It was as if we had handed the scalping knife to our most hated enemies through some misguided and manipulated sense of justice. And latter that analogy would prove very true on the battlefield at Wyoming.

It also did not bode well that Parshall Terry, of an otherwise good patriot family, remained on the hoof, as they say. He had joined up with Pa and the rest in the Independent Companies and had marched with them until one day while bending down to buckle his shoe on a forced march to escape the British in New Jersey he felt the flat of Captain Ransom's sword on his back. Now they had been fast friends before the war but that didn't mean nothing to a tired, cold, and weary Parshall Terry. He did what any man would do when insulted in such a way, he sprung to his feet and flattened Captain Ransom with a punch so square and sure to his jaw it sent him flying head over heals making the rest of 'em think he done killed him. After hurried conversations most of the others told him he best beat feet afore the other officers discovered his great breach of discipline and he did just that, getting back to Wyoming a week latter with tails of how we all was doomed and such, and didn't have much of an army from what he saw anyways, no army of any account that is. Such is a traitor's tongue as his spirit begins to fade.

The fires of war not burning quite as hot as they would latter and he stayed on in Wyoming without much fuss about him quitting the army. Especially when word come that over fifty from the two Westmoreland Companies did the same thing after the battle of Bound Brook, New Jersey, just a short while latter. Ragged, cold, and neglected by all, they figured they had done their duty as tolerably as any men could in such dire circumstances and needed some time to recover their failing health. Well General Washington personally got involved and had the remaining men of the companies fetch them back. He had a soft spot for them, for he knew of their neglected condition, and of their spirit. He admired them for it. He said of them 'men so unused to resistance must be lead, they will not be drove.' It is a hard thing to get a citizen army together, especially in a new nation such as ours, what without any tradition or nothing yet. Heck, we really didn't have a flag then. It was just a bunch of people wanting to be free to run their own affairs as they seen fit, is all. They were strong hearted men, but mostly free, and only banded together to protect their mutual freedom. They knew the necessity of rank, discipline and all, but would only tolerate the smaller bullies to organize themselves to beat the bigger bullies.

Washington recognized the free spirit in them he said, they just needed a certain understanding. When he first arrived at Cambridge to take command of the militia units the Continental Congress said would be the basis of the new army, it is said Washington was disturbed by the lack of spirit he witnessed. Some regiments would just get right up and march right out of camp and back to the farm if'n they figured some high handed fellow got too rough with them. But General Nathaniel Greene consoled the great general by saying not everyone shared his great zeal and spirit for the new idea of the country, or even saw it yet. His eyes, as well as his heart, saw well beyond most men of the day. Some things that are new just take time to develop in men's souls. Well when Captain Durkee of the Independent Companies rode from Wyoming in December of 1776 and practically begged for General Washington to let them leave Wyoming and join up with him while others were leaving like droves of flies before the plague, Washington, with a wink to Greene, said he had found men of like spirit in these Wyoming Rangers as he called them. He called them right up and they served right smart until they run out of everything. But they still stayed and fought, with the exception of Terry and a very few others. Soon their clothes were rags in the dead of winter and they, being a frontier lot, fell through the cracks when it came to supplies. They hovered around other Connecticut regiments and took their charity only so long as their pride could take it, and I guess after Bound Brook some of them a figured they had had enough for a while and set off back to Wyoming with some plunder they had acquired in the battle. Being free minded men they really thought nothing of it and swore they would return when they all recovered. Washington understood them and when they were fetched back he commuted their sentence of fifty lashes a man, and just explained he needed men of spirit with him now, especially now, for rather than ending, this whole mess was just starting. Needless to say, they all understood and I never heard of a desertion from them after that. That is what is meant by a good leader. He lead instead of brow beating the men with some trumped up speech about tradition and all. He talked to them as men of like spirit and explained, instead of just whipping and beating them. He was the good father, and they never forgot it, or him.

It puts me in mind of something that happen well after the war when some young snot of a man was spouting on about how much of a fool he thought Washington was in a tavern in Wyoming shortly after the great man had passed. Well, one of them listening was Palmer Ransom, son of Captain Ransom and drummer boy in those hard, cold, and unforgiving days of the Revolution. Being the drummer it would have been his task as a young man to have given the fifty lashes that Washington decided against some thirty years before. Those thoughts, and many other like thoughts, must have been swirling in Palmer's minds as he sat, now an old soldier sipping on some rum in a neglected corner of the tavern, all by himself with nothing but an old blanket shielding him from the cold. It must have infuriated him to hear this snot spout words about the very man whom gave him the freedom to say such things in the first place. The cold old winds of those merciless winters they endured in that war must have started to howl through his soul again, for the old soldier rose up from under the blanket with all the vigor of that young drummer boy surging through his veins. That great General's voice must have rose and echoed through his soul, making age lose all its discrepancies, for he bore down on the young snot with his cane with all the might and strength it would have took him to give all those lashes some thirty odd years before.

Calmer heads prevailed and finally pulled old Palmer away, but not afore he gave that snot the equivalency of those lashes about his bruised person. The infuriated snot demanded satisfaction in the courts and a date was set, and nearly all of Wyoming showed up to the courthouse that day. The snot, all cocky and sure of his criticisms of General Washington, started spouting them all over again with the protection of the court. Palmer sat, silent and still, still covered with that same old ratty blanket and leaning his chin on his cane. He said not a word in his own defense, though many an old patriot had to be restrained in the gallery from speaking for his defense. Well, it went on for a spell when the young judge suddenly excused himself from the bench. A highly peculiar action, a hush fell across the entire assembly, even the snot and his like hushed.

As the young judge strode to his chambers the doors opened and another man marched past him with nod. An aged man, he too struggled with a cane, much as Palmer did. A wave of gasps wisped through the courtroom as the aged man took his place at the bench and slammed the gavel down, announcing due to some unforeseen circumstances, he, being a duly sworn judge, though, retired, would be taking over this case.

The snot, recognizing the aged justice as none only than Mathias Hollenback, a fellow soldier and brother in arms to Palmer, sank down in his chair, his jaw nearly touching the floor. He did not utter another word, nor was none required from either he or Palmer.

With a scowl at the snot, and a graceful nod to a silent Palmer a still leaning his chin forward on his cane,

Hollenback announced that indeed Palmer was guilty of assault, as he himself would have been in similar circumstances, and ordered that he pay the fine of one penny before leaving this courtroom which he promptly produced from his own pocket and gave to the court officer; thus paying the fine.

With another nod he rose and bowed to Palmer and said something to the like that wisdom was lost on youth, as they had learned themselves in the dead of winter cold, shivering, and a starving for this country just some thirty odd years before when a man of all the ages explained to them all the greater meaning of their great sacrifices, and that they may be lost to the generations to come through the mists of time, but not through the camaraderie shared by he and his like, so long ago. He only hoped that certain young men would stop and listen to the whispers from the shadows of the past, for greater men may have spoken then, timeless men.

With an 'Amen' in the hushed courtroom Palmer rose, pulled the blanket tight around his person, and shuffled out the door with his cane scratching the floor. With a sharp rap of the gavel and one last scowl to the snot, Hollenback too excused himself. He passed a suddenly revived younger judge on his way to the judge's chamber's doors.

Such was the way of those great patriots in days long ago. They did take care of one another, and no old soldier in Wyoming would never tolerate a bad word spoken about General Washington after his talk to them so long ago. His words truly touched and rang through their souls, shining in their distant memories until the last one passed.

Parshall Terry broke the camaraderie, and in that he broke the spirit of the new nation, and he was never forgiven, nor will he ever be by the men of Wyoming. Treachery has no greater equal than when it is by inflicted the hand of one of your own. A sword in a familiar hand is ever so sharper.

Chapter Nine

As everyone feared, news came from upriver late in February that Lemuel Fitch and Amos York had be wisped away by the Tories, Parshall Terry having something to do with it, no doubt. A traitor is the most dangerous, for he knows his former mates the best. This is why the man Terry drew the greatest emotions from people, for most knew him, and his family, and had actually liked the man. That is why his betrayal cut the deepest into the souls of Wyoming. Before defecting to Indian Butler he had married Amy Stevens, another much liked person of Wyoming. But folks didn't blame her much, she was just being the dutiful wife. The true treachery lie with the head of their house, Parshall. A blackguard indeed.

Colonel Denison immediately raised the call for militia and it was promptly answered, mostly by the same men whom answered it in December. So off they marched in the dead of the winter up the frozen river, their frosty breaths wisping in the air as we watched them depart.

Things being as they were, much more tense than before, and the weather cold enough to freeze the teats off a cow, they only advanced as far as Wyalusing, there to rescue the York, Kingsley and Fitch families. Finding their way quite difficult when a sudden warm-up made the trail mud, they used that burgeoning sense that would become known as American ingenuity, and dismantled cabins at the Indian village to make rafts. Their fine hewed logs made quite the lumber rafts and provided a quicker way of escaping the hostile North. The unseasonably warm temperatures drew a certain angst from most of the superstitious folks of the day as they drew a liking to the warm air to the heightened passions of the British, Tories, and Indians upriver. Folks of the frontiers looked for signs and such in those days and some still do, though they are not so headstrong about it. I know many folk who will stop you from rocking an empty rocking chair as it means death in the house soon, and many a horseshoe still hang over many doors. Some things never die. It is a way to make sense of the mysterious way of things. It gives folks a feeling of control.

Mrs. York, being a most outspoken person, cussed and bantered on about the fort on her return. Her curses of Thomas Hill and Parshall Terry still ring in my ears to this day when I think on it. She never forgave them for taking her dear Amos and depriving her of a husband and her children of a father. Such were the deep emotions of the day, and the war touched all on a personal level.

Seeing how she was so destitute and all, they made her the cook for Forty Fort, seeing how a lot of folks now moved into it, leastways the ones paying heed to the signs. My grandfather being one of them. Ornery as she was, Mrs. York was a fine cook. She was the first I really seen bearing that hollow, empty, and far away look the curse of war etches into one's eyes. And it was fitting, for she did indeed lose everything. No one ever forgot about the Tory threat winging in the sky when she was about. Her sad eyes spoke for her, even when her cutting tongue did not. Such a pure heartfelt sorrow I had never seen afore. But she swore to stay on and await her Amos' return, though it proved futile in the end. Those who tried to urge her back to Connecticut failed in the face of the strong woman's faith. She developed a strong faith in the face of it all and rode many a mile in snow and sleet in her old age to attend church, saying she had awaited the arrival of Zion so long in the wilderness nothing would stop her from attending services. Oh, what those poor people went through to etch out their spot in the wilderness. Can anyone not truly living it and witnessing such heart wrenching sights ever understand? I wonder.

But the winter at Forty Fort went on without incident and come spring everyone looked from its walls for a faint glimmer of hope. Hope soon to fade. I and Will of course looked upon it all as a great adventure, and could not for the lives of us understand the grown-ups' angst. We played about the fort. It seemed such a wonder to us and we loved having free reign through the large fort. There never seemed to be a dull moment, what with all the coming and going of folks. Each carried a new story which always harbored a new fear. And with the warnings more and more folks took up in the fort. Thomas Bennett took up the middle cabin and I and Will thought it just fine, they being relation and all. He and Grandpa could weave great webs through their stories and many stopped by just to hear them. They had a way of lighting up the mood of things which was much wanting.

Something was always happening around the fort. It had two gates, one facing north and the other facing south. If nothing was happening at one gate there would be something happening at the other. Colonel Denison always seemed about taking in new reports and such and sending out dispatches directing the different companies of the 24th stationed throughout the valley from the fort, though he stayed outside its walls in his cabin along Abraham's Creek. Mother York always had a word of warning for him about the Tories every time he passed by her kitchen. She would rush out behind him a waving her spoon to the high heavens and spouting on about them. "Lord bless thee Nathan Denison!" she would always say. "For the fate of all rests with thee, so don't you forget it! Keep a sharp eye to the north, for the devil himself awaits up there! And don't you fer doubt it none!"

At first Colonel Denison would nod and smile, but soon grew tired of her, and paid her no mind until she waved her spoon in his face. Then he would say "I have things well in hand, Ms. York. Well in hand!" To which she would say "You best! You best, fine sir!" every time.

The way he would move about to avoid the kitchen proved its own sport in the end, so disturbed he became by the overbearing woman. Sometimes he would absentmindedly stumble past the kitchen in deep thought and break into a run to avoid the waving spoon of Mother York.

I and Will would climb up to the ladders to the low platform running all along the walls and watch the spectacles with a keen interest. Every day held its own entertainment and sport. Oh, to be a child again. Along some sides of the double-hewed logged walls they simply used the cabin roofs as the platform and we would hear a scolding from below each time I and Will would scamper along them to find some new excitement brewing somewhere below the walls, inside and out. For many gathered outside the walls to conduct business and just meet now and then. The fort became the unofficial center of everything in the valley in those days. I guess folks drew a sense of security from it. It was quite a sight, and looking back I often wonder why all of us simply did not just wait in the fort for the Indians and Tories to tire from their raid and leave. For I tell you they never would have taken it without a battery of strong cannon.

Its walls stood a full forty feet from the ground, made with hewn lumber posts stacked double thick and stood upright in six foot trenches. Four bastions sat at each corners which rose another six feet. Inside it had a forge, kitchen, magazine, stables, and many cabins along with root cellars full of provisions. A barricaded tunnel led to a spring near the river from its east wall. Its green was well over a acre in the middle of it. Yes, even without cannon, for we had only one, a four pound cannon, which stayed at Wilkes-Barre Fort, it proved formidable and the best of all the forts in the entire valley. I tell you I and Will were very found and proud of it as were most in the valley those days. But pride can be a fickle thing and can lead otherwise smart men astray. Such is what I believe happened at the great battle that was yet to happen. For pride was one sense every Wyoming man had in abundance.

That is why moments which shake that great sense of pride are remembered while others may fade. One such incident etched itself forever in my mind in those carefree days before the battle. Colonel Denison sent many scouts upriver to try and catch some early warning of the mischief thereabouts that spring before the battle. Some say at the behest of Mother York's spoon and sharp tongue. But that is neither here nor there. Colonel Denison would have done it without the threat of the 'spoon.' It just urged things on a bit more smartly.

Needless to say, few scouts dared brave the wilderness above Tunkhannock Creek, for they would have certainly lost their hair. One such scout, carried out by a man named Crooks and his friend Budd carried back a harbinger of things to come which would bring sober the most vague mind. At least it did for I and Will, for we never seen such a look in a man's eyes before that horrible battle when such a look became commonplace.

Crooks and Budd took a canoe up to Tunkhannock to check out the abandoned place of John Secord, for it was a right smart place before he run up to Tioga Point. Secord, being a known Tory, was certain to never return. Such were the emotions in those days. Well Crook always had a keen eye for land and a eye for Secord's place and now had the opportunity to claim it as his own for after the war. He was a casting his eye right proud over the land from the doorway of Secord's own home when several balls cut his view short. He collapsed immediately to the floor to breathe no more, much to the angst of Budd standing but a few feet away. Some say it was a raiding party under James Secord, John's son, who led the Tory and Indian raiding party that day. Such is God's sense of justice, mysterious indeed. It just goes to show you how near danger dwelt to the front door of Wyoming. For in all truth the Tories controlled over two thirds of it, from Tioga down to Tunkhannock. Only the large population centers of the lower settlements kept them at bay. And they would soon attend to that problem.

Budd lit out like the devil himself was chasing him. And he was, in the form of painted men wearing feathers, screaming and howling close to his heels. Running for all get out, he leaped rail fences and flew through the forest, turning to fire his one shot and throw his rifle at the demons afore scrambling on for dear life. He said all he could think on was getting to the river and finding their canoe, for death breathed heavy down his neck. He said he never prayed so much in his life than when being chased by those howling and painted red men. Demons in the like, he called them.

Somehow he stumbled down the riverbank with his hair still atop his head and tumbled into their canoe, fearing all the while he had busted through the bottom of the frail craft. He pushed it out into the current with madly flailing arms and didn't stop until he made it back to Forty Fort, praising God and praying all the way through that long night.

It just so happen that I and Will was up and about afore sunrise and was one of the first to see him pull up his canoe at the landing below the fort. Sensing something was askew by the way he walked and bantered on about Injuns, we ran up to him along with the sentry about the gate.

Budd walked wide-eyed past the sentry still ranting about the Indians when he caught the attention of Colonels Butler and Denison. He noticed them, but kept right on past them with us boys tailing him. "Boys, I wish fer all get out your folks would take heed and fetch you all out of this afore it's too late," he said within ear shot of the two colonels. "After all, it's only ground, there's always plenty more of it, but life, that's precious and beyond all, and men will take it for land and such, the most precious gift of life. And I tell you there's a bunch a comin' fer this land!" He stopped afore his cabin door and shook his head afore opening the door. He wasted no time in grabbing his traps and such and waved his hand to us boys standing in the doorway. "You boys help me with some of this?" he asked, holding up some bundles of furs.

We both nodded. Eagerly grabbing them we slung them over our shoulders, glad to be officially included in the ruckus causing everyone around the fort to gather. We followed him out the door but this time his tongue remained silent. He just marched headlong for the gate, ignoring all the questioning eyes cast his way. His own eyes bore a glared over solid look of dread. He grunted and shifted his heavy load of traps, bundles, and such, for he carried all in the world he owned, but he offered no more advice to anyone.

The colonels suddenly strode forth and incepted us just afore the gate, standing just off to the side of us. Seeing how Budd didn't even nod his head to them, Denison said "Budd, come now, man, what has happened?"

Budd stopped dead in his tracks and I and Will nearly plowed into his backside it was so abrupt. Right then and there he dropped his traps and spouted out his whole story for all to hear, clear and loud in that hushed fort. Not even a whisper sounded to interrupt him, but all listened with a sharp ear.

The colonels stood and listened patiently, as the gentlemen they were, but could not help but roll an eye to one another from time to time. Just as Budd stopped and bent down to pick up his traps Denison raised his hand towards him and said, "come man, come to your senses. Sit for a spell and rest, let your mind clear of its horrors and you shall be able to think right of the situation."

"Think right!?!" Budd gasped. "I durst think I have never thought clearer in my life! I tell you my good Colonel all of hell is a floating down that river, painted, wearing green and red jackets they is! All full and hell bent on a clearing out this here valley! It's God's honest truth! And now poor Crooks has breathed his last because of it!" He turned and looked away from the colonels shakin' their heads and gazed all around. "It's only land!" he screamed. "There's always more of it! But once your life is gone it's gone!"

"Come now!" Denison said. "It is much more than that! The lifeblood of which you speak runs in this very soil! Our soil! We have braved many hazards to secure it and shall not falter in the face of this overblown challenge!"

"Overblown my arse!" Budd said. "I getting out, and anyone in his right mind will do the same, fine sir!" With that he picked up his traps and marched headlong to the canoe, stopping just long enough to load it and give us boys a nod afore paddling down the river. I never saw a more determined look on anyone's face than on his that day.

Some in the fort stepped out and watched his canoe

slowly disappear down the river, each as silent as the next. The colonels themselves strode up the bank and watched until well after the canoe drifted out of sight. I and Will watched them for the longest time. They just stood there, Denison a rubbing his chin, and Butler a standing there with one hand cocked on his hip. They stared, deep in thought, once in while turning to look up at the sea of silent faces staring over the fort's walls. I tell you it give me the willies, but neither me or Will spoke a word through it all, so imposing it was.

Finally, as the sun teased the tops of the west mountains, the colonels both turned an eye to one anther and marched back to the fort, sharing careful and hushed whispers between them. All that night and into the next day things stayed quiet, with only occasional small talk passing between everyone. I tell you things like that touch the innocents such as children, for none of us raised more than a whisper until the dread Budd so artfully described faded with time. Then that great spirit emerged in everyone's hearts again, coupled with the grim determination which brought them into these far mountains nestled in the wilderness in the first place. No, they would not be denied their sacred right of soil, for in the end it was the life of which Budd spoke. Let him be off, to each his own. But the Wyoming settlers would stand fast, for their own lives and their posterity. For their land was their life.

Chapter Ten

It's sometimes hard to think about the good things in the normal turn of life in such pressing times, but one has only to look, and somehow those things do shine through the darkest gloom. Such was the Jenkins' wedding just afore all hell broke loose in Wyoming. Somehow, as I recall, it did have a calming effect on some tense souls in those days, and did tame the angst in everyone's heart, if for but a fleeting moment. It may have had something to do with Johnny Jenkins popping out of the forest just a few weeks afore the battle. Folks around Fort Jenkins stood stunned, even his own folks, when that skeleton of a man appeared as if from the depths of hell itself. It wasn't that folks had given up hope, but the last they heard he was put in a cold dark hole in Fort Niagara; a special little place the misplaced Tories of Wyoming in Indian Butler's ranks reserved for the Wyoming Yankee's alone. Those Butler's Rangers were the bane of Wyoming, and we had a special place in their hearts, a special place in a most bad way.

When I first saw Johnny, I must admit, I was scared of him. He didn't appear nothing like the man I knew afore he was captured and put in that hell at Niagara. Gaunt, ghostly, and pale is how I mostly remember him, and as a child we first avoided him like the plague, but his charm was not lacking, and he seemed to become accustomed to the horrible stares of shock cast at him from afar by most folks upon meeting him again. Poor Will hung behind me and peered around me as if using me as a shield against the devil. But Johnny, a man not big on words, but one accustomed to action, marched right up to us in his ill-fitting clothes that had fit him fine just a few months afore, and knelt down face to face to us, nodding his head and patting us on the shoulders. Even Will lost his fear staring into those hollow, but welcoming eyes, somehow recognizing that familiar essence which was Johnny Jenkins' alone. Once you were his friend, you were his friend, for all of life, unless you turned Tory or such, that is. This we recognized without a word and our fear melted. Then all we saw was a bit more aged and ragged Johnny Jenkins afore us, but Johnny Jenkins, for sure. I tell you men of those times shone with a certain radiance that has somehow been lost, whether God himself inhabited the men then for that special time in history or not, I don't know. It's just to say I ain't never witnessed such a light shinning from men's souls as I did in those days. They all had it, God bless them they did, and sometimes I pray hard to God to infest men with such a spirit again, but alas, as the times are now lost in the past, so seems that spirit. That true American spirit has never shone quite as brilliant as when it was first born, strange as it was. And Johnny Jenkins had it in spades. We all cared for one another and seemed to realize the importance of just what was happening, more for just us living in that day, but for those whom would live the many days and untold generations after us. All men should have that spirit, and I tell you it sure seems lacking in the day I write this, many years after the fact. But such are the failings of man, he seems to need to fall backwards to gain a great step forwards, or needs to cast himself into the darkness just to hunger for the brighter light of a new day. Strange, man is, strange indeed.

But Johnny Jenkins, kneeling down to us scared boys, let all I have mentioned shine through his eyes, somehow. I care, those eyes said. And you need not fret or wonder on it, here stands your friend, now and forever, in this time and beyond. That is how strong that spirit was, it didn't need any words, but some high sounding men sure found them in their shinning declarations. Such times. Such men.

Another come up besides Johnny there on his wedding day at Fort Jenkins on that late June day afore all the world crumbled and went up in flames around us, and she shared his silent charm, along with a graceful beauty few possess or ever witness. Bethiah Harris was easily one of the most beautiful women I have ever seen, and to this day I still recollect her smile and must confess it does touch my heart, even after all these years. She truly possessed a timeless beauty and charm.

She smiled, recognizing the fear Johnny's smile had chased away from our hearts. She nodded to both of us, saying, "it's alright now, young un's, it's Johnny, and he's come back, makes faith shine all the more, it does for sure."

Johnny smiled at her and said, "there she be boys, a good woman with a good heart, and I tell you I carried her hope with me all through my terrible ordeal. A woman's love boys, it's worth coveting and cherishing, and in the end one of the most pure things there is, got me through hell itself it did. So boys, find yourself such and your life will be all the more richer." Beth smiled at him and beamed with a radiance born of pure love. "That's why I promised myself to marry her as soon as I got back, come hell or high water, no matter what my social situation, for being through hell puts one in the proper perspective, it does fer sure," Johnny added.

With that, he rose from us boys and faced the silent crowd gathering around the fort. All hushed and stood stunned, for they had listened to his words. He patted us both on the head and we both hugged him, in spite of everyone else watching. Beth joined him, and arm in arm, they turned, both grinning from ear to ear. The whole crowd suddenly cheered, with the reverend announcing with his booming voice all is well this day, regardless of the Tory and Indian threat, and this day would shine with a light born of pure love, no one could doubt it.

Johnny and Beth both moved to a spot in the middle of the crowded fort and stood in front of the reverend spreading his hands out as to present them. Johnny, though a skeleton of a man, rose tall and stout, jutting his chest and beaming with a radiance born of the pure love he found and shared with his equally beaming bride.

The reverend raised his hands high and slowly lowered them, pulling his good book from the inside pocket of his black coat. Then, of course, he spouted those coveted words all preachers love to say; out come the ring Johnny himself had forged just afore the wedding, and then, the good reverend, with a smile equal to the bride and groom's, proudly announced them man and wife.

They both kissed, long and hard, with everyone standing silent in awe. True love, when its shines, has that effect on people, out of envy, or perhaps, awe. I tell you it sure helped to ease the tense and foreboding air of those days.

Out come John Murphy with a bread peel, as was the custom then, for every new bride was presented one, and he smartly presented it to the truly blushing, but beaming, bride. He turned, beaming with pride, back to the crowd. They burst with cheers.

The ensuing celebration is still fondly remembered by those still living whom witnessed it, after all these years, such as it was. Folks seem to live in an intensity and a welcoming heart when threatened so, as we were by the storm of war blowing down our necks. I myself still live with the memories, good and bad, of those days, though I was so young. I tell you I can remember those days more than I can remember what happened just yesterday in these days long passed, as I write this. It is the intensity of the times. One never lives more and feels more than when threatened with losing the greatest gift of all, life. Even as a boy it touched me, and I think if looked upon in the true importance of the day and in the overall life of this nation, it truly shines in the annals of the nation.

Such times, such people, should never be forgotten, for they lived in the intensity of the uncertain birth of this nation. And a nation's true light never shines brighter than in the innocence of its birth, pure and simple, before it is clouded by the complications of further life. That is why we should always look back to them, whom not only shined in the purity and innocence of the nation's birth, but actually witnessed it. There is nothing like a first hand account of things, be they good or bad.

Chapter Eleven

Life is constant, in all times, new or old, full or dull, and the certain peculiarities of life remain constant also, such as my predicament soon after Johnny's wedding. The body's wants are constant, regardless of man's complications and conflicts. Daily life will go on, regardless. Bodies will be plagued with certain aliments, such as toothaches. And let me tell you after Johnny's wedding, perhaps from partaking in too many sweet delicacies, my jaw throbbed something fierce.

Grandpa, sick of my moaning, much as Ma, took matters into their own hands. After tying a cord around my tooth and trying the door thing, which I durst say did nothing more than to make me cry all the more, Grandpa decided upon a particular remedy which drew fame to Wyoming in those days. Seems one of our stout souls, being plagued by a aching tooth himself, and being far from the care of any doctor or such, took matters in his own hands. Being all by himself, he fashioned his own remedy by a certain method which proved most effective, and I for one can tell you is a legend born of truth, for I experienced it first hand. Well, this stout soul carved a notch in a rifle ball and tied a cord to it. Attaching the other end to his tooth he rammed the ball, figuring it to be the most powerful thing around, down his rifle and fired it, thus, releasing him from the cause of his agonizing pain. Amazed, he bragged about his method all over Wyoming, where the strange, but effective method, became known as pulling a Wyoming tooth, or simply the Wyoming tooth when word spread further on, as such strange practices will be known.

When Grandpa took his rifle down from the mantle and grabbed me, moaning and crying, up by the neck, I must admit I did fret a bit. He paid me no mind and pulled me out the door to the yard, with Will, Ma, and Grandma at his heels, all watching in amazement. Waving his hand to hush my protesting Ma, Grandpa pulled his long knife and notched out a ball in front of me. I remember I suddenly stopped moaning, but it did me no good, for Grandpa seemed most determined.

After notching the ball real careful like, he pulled out an old hemp cord and attached one end to my aching tooth and the other to the ball. I'll never forget Will's eyes shining up at me in wonder. His eyes seemed full of questions, but he did not speak. He hovered around Grandpa and followed him a few steps away after Grandpa felt he secured the cord tight enough around my aching, but stubborn, tooth. I watched Will's wondrous eyes gleam up at the rifle while Grandpa rammed the ball carefully home, as he had turned his back to me.

Ma come up and held me by the shoulders. Grandma stood beside her with her hands cupped to her slackened jaw. Neither said a word, but just watched, seeming to be as full of wonder as Will. I must say I did not share their certain curiosity, but its partner, fear. Still I stood rigid and still watching Grandpa raise his rifle. I opened my mouth wide and braced myself, feeling Ma's hand slowly pass over my eyes in the fatal moment of my tooth.

With a loud bang, a cloud of smoke, and a quick tug, my pain disappeared and I pushed Ma's hand away to see Will gawking at me and Grandpa looking down at me with raised eyebrows. Ma twirled me around and forced my mouth wide open. Watching her eyes draw wide in amazement made my heart rise full in its chest. It worked! By jingo it worked!

No one seemed gladder to hear the news than Grandpa. With beaming eyes he looked down at his rifle and said, "damnedest thing I ever heard tell of, but it sure works, God help me, it works, and I reckon a might smart better than old Hooker Smith's pliers at that!"

Ma ushered me into the house and put a wet cloth to my bleeding jaw when a sudden commotion outside drew us both out the door again. The gasps from Grandma drew us out the door all the faster. Her stunned face turning back to us made us stop on the porch and gaze at the panting man standing by Grandpa and Will.

"It's terrible!" the man managed to say through pants, "I knew 'em well, myself, and knew the man Quocko to be a friend of yours, so I come as soon as I heard!"

Grandpa shook his head and staggered back to the porch. Easing his rifle down onto the edge of it, he slowly sat down, his mouth agape.

"They got Quocko!" Will explained to me and Ma. "They got Quocko!"

"Ma'am," the panting messenger said, trying to slow his breaths. The distant boom of the cannon at Wilkes-Barre Fort echoed through the silent air. Something had, or was, happening, but I and Ma couldn't seem to get a word out of anyone, save Will. Ma stepped up to the messenger and took him by the shoulders, recognizing the booming cannon as the call for the militia to form up in the forts. Another echo suddenly sounded in the distance-the strong beat of a drum.

"They got the whole Harding party upriver!" the messenger said, stepping away to the sound of the approaching drum. "Colonel Denison's called up the 24th!" he added, seeming to be drawn to the sound of the drum coming up the road. Ma's eyes grew just as wide as Grandma's and Grandpa's. She shook her head in disbelief.

"I just stopped to tell you Quocko Martin was took along with the rest, at least that's what young Hadsall says, he stumbled into Fort Jenkins just this morning with a horrible tale, he did at that," the messenger said, giving me an odd look before scampering off to the road. I took the wet rag from my mouth and stared at the splotches of blood on it. I too gasped in horror, thinking hard on dear Quocko's fate. Oddly, I thought of how the news would effect far off Pa fighting somewhere out there for his country to restrain the forces of a tyrant whose forces now came a callin' at his own doorstep.

The echo of the far off drum quickly grew until it seemed to thunder its call of war to our very doorstep at the lead of a right smart column. Colonel Denison had wasted no time. He not only called up the militia, but had them marching right in front of us to go and settle this question. A hundred or so stern-faced souls marched right behind he and Colonel

Butler, both sitting high and straight in their saddles, their hard eyes staring straight up the road. Grandma gasped all the more and gripped a post on the porch. Her eyes fell to Grandpa, but she seemed too crippled with fright to step towards him.

Grandpa glanced at her out of the corner of his eye and quickly rose, straightening his powder horn and pouch. His white knuckles gripped his rifle.

"No!" Grandma gasped, reaching a hand out in the air between them. "They have enough men!" she gasped. "More than enough! Besides, it's young men's work! Men young of heart!"

"My heart is as young as the next, though my bones may not be," Grandpa said, giving her a quick nod afore marching towards the column. "A man's got to do what he is called to do!"

"Pa, wait on a minute!" Ma suddenly said, chasing behind him.

"Now get back on the porch now, dear Lois," Grandpa said, turning back to her and all of us. "We need all dutiful women and children now, as well as men. I must go! So just mind yourself and tend to matters as they may present themselves. Get everyone to the fort!"

"But Pa, Ma is right!" Ma said.

"No, she is not," Grandpa simply said, turning and joining the column of stern-faced men.

Ma did not argue, but turned and gathered us into the cabin, telling us to quickly collect all we could for our stay at the fort, for she had no idea how long it would be.

With Grandpa's words echoing in our ears we dutifully obeyed, though Grandma did with great tears. All the world seemed to be closing in on us, and nothing we seemed to do could alter it. It fell heavily on all our souls, and even I found it hard to breath in the face of the great unknown threat descending upon our little settlement in the wilderness.

But then Grandpa returned, upon order of Denison..

Chapter Twelve

A strange air of excitement filled the fort. A hollow, strong, but odd feeling, as I recall. It is hard to describe unless one feels it himself. It is a strange combination of fear and curiosity, as if you know the devil is knocking at your door and you don't want to open it, but a voice haunts your soul just to open it a crack and take a look at the awful demon. I tell you, do not open the door! But, alas, Wyoming never turned its back on a challenge, or a threat. A blessing, and a curse.

Grandpa led us right through the mingling masses to the cabin next to Thomas Bennett, a relation. To his great relief, he found it unoccupied and put a claim to it straight away, first come, first served, and all.

Grandma and Ma took to setting up housekeeping straight away, but me, Grandpa, and Will were drawn to the hubbub inside the fort like a magnet to steel. The woman folk always busied themselves in such times. I reckon it eased their minds to be busy. As Ma always said, idle hands are the devil's workshop. She took it to heart. But as for us men, and boys, curiosity rose above all our senses. If something bad approached we wanted to know about it and stare in straight in the face. Grandpa always said it's best to stare your enemy right in the face when he approaches, and be quick to strike afore he can get set. Many Wyoming men felt the same, as their latter actions proved.

Every soul in Wyoming seemed to be hovering about, talking, gathering, loading supplies, and such. Everyone shared a hollow, empty look. Then some boisterous soul announced to all Wyoming could stand anything! We had proved it time and time again! Stand strong ye men of Wyoming! I tell you I heard it every fifteen minutes or so as folks tried to reassure themselves against their growing angst.

Seeing as Connecticut has a strong sea-faring element, Colonel Butler himself owned three sea-going vessels, and we had many an old sea captain among us, most notably, Captain Carr, whom took over the ninth, or upriver company after John Secord's defection to the Tory side of things. From his like many old sea-faring songs blared in the air; for many always found music a tonic, and many found need for a strong tonic in such tense times, be it drink or song.

The tin whistles and such drew I and Will to them and Grandpa to many huddled group of concerned citizens gathering about to discuss their predicament over a mug of rum. It's not that everyone was a drunk, but the quality of water being such in those days, people took to drinking, for it seemed to be the only safe thing to drink. I and Will was both raised on small beer, rum, and hard cider, but it never did me no harm, as folks claim in this day I write. The women of the temperance movement would find no allies in those days, for everyone drank out of necessity, from the preacher to the youngest infant. Perhaps that had something to do with the spirit of the day.

I and Will hovered about the smaller circles of people. Seeming to be overlooked in such times, we took full advantage of the situation and saw and heard everything. Will sat mesmerized by Captain Carr singing one old song after another while he cleaned his rifle, or sharpened his long knife on a wet-stone. I traveled from one group to the next, listening in wonder of all. Most all felt certain of their capabilities and took to heart that call, stand strong ye men of Wyoming. Many repeated it after they heard it called.

It seemed almost a festival, a great gathering of everyone about Wyoming, and in some of the huddled groups took on such a meaning after the rum flowed more freely. Ma never called us back to the cabin, and her only warning was to stay within the walls of Forty Fort and out from underfoot. So I hovered around with this boy and that, all of us barefoot, as was the custom in the summer for children and women. To us it seemed the greatest of adventures, and somehow we knew we were witnessing a great history unfolding right afore our eyes. And we was part of it. Such adventures of which boys only dream, we lived. But beware, for some adventures turn into nightmares in the end, such as this one.

But we still stared in awe and wonder of every little drama playing about, until one in particular overshadowed all. Everyone suddenly turned towards a call from the gate, not to stand strong, but to stand ready. All us boys, along with everyone else, clambered to the gate, some up to the platforms below the walls, and others to the crowded gate itself, only to reluctantly part to let Colonel Denison and his men enter.

Denison enter silently at first, his eyes staring far off in some deep thought, afore he turned them down to recognize the many questioning eyes looking up to him. Many clamored around the equally sullen men following him. All bore that same hollow gaze which seemed to haunt their souls, making their hearts heavy as well as their tongues. When one finally did mumble a few words to one of their nagging women folk the word spread through us like thunder. The Harding Party had been massacred!

Men and women alike stood hushed by the full weight of the awful news. All followed Denison to the middle of the fort and glared up at him, their stern eyes demanding an explanation, though their tongues remained silent.

Denison finally reined his horse about and stared glumly down at the sea of eyes. "We have been struck, it is true," he announced. "We have recovered some of the slain and have laid them to rest about Fort Jenkins." He paused for a moment and looked sternly down at the shocked eyes below him. "Others are missing, we no not of their fate, hopefully, they shall return on their own accord. But we must not lose face, but stay strong! The first blow may have been struck! We ourselves have dispatched two of the devils lying in wait to ambush our very number! Let us hope our actions prove to our brazen foe our stern intentions and they turn about, if not we shall meet them, and drive them out of our valley!"

A series of loud cheers answered his declaration. He nodded to each of the beaming eyes now shinning through the former gloom in his heart and answered each rousing huzza with his own. He promptly dismounted and strode straight towards Thomas Bennett's cabin, calling for his officers in his wake. All the assembled officers dutifully followed, along with throngs of us curious folks scampering behind them. We all hovered about the open door and windows, silently listening to ever word. Whispers flowed from those close to the windows and throughout the crowd.

With the final announcement from Denison that he intended to stand fast against any threat against our beloved soil, a great cheer arose from the crowd. Some tense folks, mostly older people, urged a bit of caution, only to be quickly shunned by the enthusiasm cursing through the crowd.

None cheered louder than Lazarus Stewart, our hero, sauntering through the gate in the lead of his Hanover Boys at the last moment. His great enthusiasm touched everyone. He had that certain air and absolute belief in our cause in spades. I believe no one had a higher confidence in our new nation, and himself. To us boys this impetuous, clever, and strong man proved the model of the American frontiersman. No sir, nothing would stop him, nor his country, once he, or it, set its mind to something.

Colonel Denison apparently heard his friend's booming and rather unique voice. He burst through the door and crowd to meet him with a great embrace and a solid embrace. Everyone cheered all the more. Wyoming did indeed stand tall, and solid. Woe be to any Tory or Indian fool enough to tromp on this soil with an eye to conquering it. It would indeed prove a fool's folly, and their last act!

Even though our hero had resigned his commission as Lieutenant Colonel of the *Twenty-fourth* a while ago, everyone still followed him as if he still retained the rank, and listened to him in that respect. Disgruntled and disillusioned with the quivering command, as he called it, of the regiment, he had even politely refused the captaincy offered to him by the Hanover Boys for their company, preferring to be but a mere private. But such are the failings of proper rank, sometimes the best men wait in the shadows. Even the true captain of the Hanover Company, Captain Mckarrachan, deferred to Lazarus from time to time. Besides, folks on the frontier didn't take much to proper title and all. If their came a call for them to get together most times they elected their true leaders right then and there, despite what the proper people told them.

Such a man strode up and embraced the two men, Stephen Harding, called captain out of respect by most of us, even though when he occupied the ranks in the independent companies he had only the *proper* rank of private. He too held our respect in spades. Sometimes the proper folks don't understand the collective intelligence of the common folk, but such it has always been and shall always be, Wyoming was no exception, though Colonel Denison was a fine man in all respects.

With Lazarus's blessing, Denison turned to the other officers, ordering them to prepare for the defense of our beloved valley. He sent men to all parts with the call to assemble to meet the British tyrant's and his savage hordes' threat.

Everyone spread out, all invigorated and confident they could match any threat thrown at them. After all, to them simple justice lay with their cause, and thus Providence.

To us young ones it seemed the whole world suddenly seemed to be turning on its axis around us in that huddled fort. We all scampered around to watch the many dramas playing about us in preparation for war. Men hovered over barrels of powder, filling their horns. Grinding wheels twirled to the force of strong-armed men, sharpening many a blade from tomahawk to long knife. Women rolled cartridges, their nimble fingers being the best at such things. Mrs. York cooked over large pots in her kitchen, grinning and smiling from ear to ear. More rifles and muskets appeared than we had ever seen afore in our lives. It all seemed so real, so intense.

As the fading light fell over the walls we boys scampered to the north gate, there to stare out into the waning light of day settling over the trees beyond. For a moment our imaginations flared with horrible visions of red painted and green coated men marching stalwartly from the shadows of the trees. Hundreds of painted men dashed and darted about our soldiers' flanks, all screaming and yelling their blood-curling wails. But then the booming voice of our hero echoed through our minds, forever vanquishing the horrid visions back into the darkness whence they came. His confidence proved contagious, even to us young boys.

We all turned toward the booming voice and then rolled our eyes back to the gate. The descending darkness no longer harbored gloom, but hope. We saw beyond the shadows to the new day beyond. The day when the unbroken forest would be tamed forever and a new forest, of sturdy homes and buildings, would dominate the horizon. We saw that all, too. We saw the hope of the future for which our elders now gathered for war to defend and establish. They took the first steps and somehow we felt a certain obligation to see their visions through to fruition.

Such was our task, but for now we stared across the fields in front of the forest which we knew as playgrounds, and the scene of many imaginary battles, and felt the hope of a new day, past this horrid one, well past.

Suddenly we noticed the gentle flecks of fireflies dancing smoothly on the summer breezes over the fields in the twilight. The descending shadows did not seem so threatening, but peaceful as home. Our blessed home.

We felt certain Providence blessed us pioneers, we blazing the trails across the virgin land to create something new among man, a new nation, an American nation.

Oh, to breath the free air of innocence again before the horrors of war forever darkened and tainted it.

Chapter Thirteen

With the call of adventure rattling at the door few managed to gain but a few hours sleep, especially we young ones. We rose well before the sun and snuck out of the cabins, careful not to awake any of our folks and have them spoil our fun. We quickly gathered in little groups and scampered along Captain Hewlett's scouts departing before dawn. Some of them cast a nervous smile down at us filing along side of them to the gate, while most just stared blankly ahead, their minds and thoughts on their task of discovery. But we cheered them on nonetheless and climbed the ladders to the platforms below the walls to watch them slowly spread out and disperse into the trees beyond, wishing all along to hear the sharp report of their rifles or such excitement soon.

We stood breathless watching them over the pointed logs, some on tiptoes, but all focused intently on the forest beyond the walls when a loud noise from behind made us all nearly jump out of our skins. We all fell from the tops of the logs and sat aghast, looking up at the grinning culprit hovering over us.

Dan Washburn, the sentry, fumbled with his long musket, struggling to suppress a great laugh building in his chest. It wouldn't do proper for a sentry to be laughing in such tense times, not even this young soul, barely older than many of the curious boys he had startled. Dan finally chuckled in spite of himself, glancing out of the corner of his eye to see if his playful acts caught the eye of the ever-present corporal of the guard. He only noticed the shaking head of a man walking to the gate below.

"What you got their Dan?" the man said with a grin. "A true lot of miscreants as I ever saw afore, indeed!"

Dan nodded to Captain Harding quickly stopping and waving his finger up to us stunned boys. "You young'uns mind your manners now, we need all good and dutiful children, as well as men, about now!" he said before marching out the gate, his eyes also full of purpose. So full, his intense stare cut through the pale light of dawn creeping over the walls. "This is the day," he called behind him, almost on a whisper ,but loud enough for us all to hear in the silent dawn. "Indeed it is!"

"You young'uns best stay out from under foot," Dan said, suddenly full of soldiery manners and standing tall. His eyes rolled from us to the long bayonet glistening in the early morning light from the end of his cumbersome firearm. It seemed to draw a haunting look to his face. He turned without another word and marched his post along platform again, his mind now solely upon his duty.

We boys stood silent and stared at one another for the longest moment before tumbling down the ladders again to the awakening fort. We soon found ourselves lost in the growing hustle and bustle of the high-spirited fort. The glowing and confident faces about us reestablished our sense of security and we soon played about again, awaiting the promise of adventure with anxious hearts once more, until a rush about the gate drew us to it.

A growing tumult spread from the clusters of settlers gathering around the onrushing scouts. Men scampered up to them and then dispersed in every direction, quickly spreading their news. Apprehension grew from every word they shouted.

Colonel Denison hurried from the Bennett cabin all in a fuss, marched steadily towards the scouts with a stern eye and sharp tongue, warning them to report to him first afore everyone else. The scouts tongues' immediately fell silent, especially when their own captain rushed urgently through the gate behind them, cradling one of his hastily bandaged and bleeding hands. He interceded between the advancing colonel and his men, stepping smartly and standing at attention just afore the colonel.

"Wintermoot's fallen, sir!" he gasped, passing his long rifle to a man near him to continue to tighten the bandage around his hand. "Indian Butler is about Exeter and may be threatening Fort Jenkins as we speak!"

Denison reared back from the news to the gasps

sounding from the hushed crowd encircling him. He stood aghast, rubbing his chin and fingering the hilt of his sword.

"One of them blistered me," Hewlett continued, seeing the colonel offer him no resistance. All should hear of the hordes threatening them. It was the New England way, what with the town meetings and all. Looking back, I am certain he felt everyone had a stake in it, so everyone should hear. "They took Sam Finch, and seem to be growing in number, sir," Hewitt added, grimacing as a woman helped him with his wounded hand.

The fear prevailing earlier immediately grew into a very real panic. Women gasped and put their hands to their cheeks. A look of absolute terror rolled across the assembled faces of the crowd, even us boys. We suddenly cowered from the wave of fear descending over the fort and sought out our parents and such, seeking their security.

Denison raised his hands, seeming bereft of any words. Other men did not seem so tongue-tied. They immediately started gathering their weapons and called for an immediate march on the enemy. This was unheard of! Are we all to just set here safe in this fort while our lands are being ravaged by the evil hordes of the villainous British Empire!?! No sir! Not these men! Not these brave men of Wyoming!

Denison immediately found his tongue, yelling for all to just calm down, for only a fool acts without thinking! This was war! Calmer heads must prevail to avoid disaster!

All us boys wondered of our hero whom had left with the rest of the Hanover Boys last night to head back to their homes in Hanover Township. They said they wished to be about their own cabins in case some stray and wild Indians should strike on their own. A dozen rogue warriors could burn a cabin and lift a scalp in the blinking of an eye. And they intended to keep their eyes wide open to their threat!

"An express!" Denison yelled, turning to Lieutenant Colonel Dorrance, a fine looking man in his finely tailored and immaculate uniform. Everyone appeared underdressed next to him, especially Denison with his disheveled hair and hunting shirt. "Send immediate expresses to Captains Franklin, Clingman, and Mckarrachan! Send word to Colonel Butler at Wilkes-Barre Fort and call in the Lackawanna Company! We must gather now! Now! Here at Forty Fort!" Denison ordered.

His orders did little to quell the growing panic, but only hastened it. Women gathered their children close. Ma appeared from nowhere and grabbed both I and Will up by the collar, herding us towards the cabin while Grandpa grabbed his rifle and headed towards the other men gathering about the gate, much to Colonel Denison's disgust.

Denison clamored through the tumultuous crowds. Finally squeezing through the crowd, he climbed a ladder and stood full on the platform just above the north gate. Raising his hands, he yelled for all to hear and calm down. Calm heads must prevail or all would be lost! Suddenly he seemed to recognize the price of popular sovereignty. Crowds ran on impulses. Impulses lead by emotions. Hasty emotions always led to disaster. You could see the fright in his eyes and I swear his voice cracked from his own emotions a couple of times afore he seemed to buck up in the face of the real threat descending over the masses.

In the face of diminishing common sense the call of cowardice rang through the crowd, no doubt directed at Colonel Denison along with many other expletives, none complimentary in nature in the least.

"That is enough!" Denison finally screamed. "I am in command, and duly elected, I might add! And if you wish my council any longer, and my leadership, I suggest ye all listen! There are no cowards in these ranks, I durst say! None!"

Another great hush slowly blanketed the crowd at the sight of an almost frantic man on the platform. Seeing one of their respectable and leading citizens threaten to come apart afore everyone's eyes seemed to have a calming effect in itself. Soon no curses or threats assaulted the air, that is, but from the direction of the kitchen. There pans clanged about and a quick tongue cursed all Tories, especially Parshall Terry. The name of this particular person drew the most ire from most folks souls, seeing how he deserted our own ranks and joined the hated Tories. Mrs. York thundered from the kitchen to investigate the growing silence with her great wooden spoon raised high over head and her sharp tongue still blaring its hateful oaths. She turned her glaring eye to the colonel staring down at her and blanched. "What's this all about!?! She finally gasped, raising her spoon towards the frustrated colonel. He looked to be fit to be tied.

"It is about sanity amidst mayhem," Denison immediately answered, regaining his composure. "It is about common sense prevailing over our wild emotions!!"

"That is well and fine," a voice in the crowd countered, "but what is war but all emotion!"

"War," Denison said, raising his arms to calm the crowd. "Is indeed all emotion. That is why those leading must not be led into its trap! We must think, man! And prepare!"

"What of Fort Jenkins!?!" another voice demanded. "It may be falling as we stand here bickering!"

"I have sent Stephen Harding there just this morning to ascertain their situation," Denison answered. "He should be returning soon and answer own concerns!"

A forthcoming scout answered the man's question in Denison's ear before he spoke another word. Everyone watched the scout whisper and awaited with breathless anticipation. Denison's eyes fell in deep thought and he again gripped the hilt of his sword. "Fort Jenkins has fallen," he said, raising his head. "But the inhabitants have been spared as of yet!"

"As of yet indeed!" a voice boomed back at him from the crowd.

"Be that as it may, we must ready ourselves!" Denison said, slamming one of his fists into his open palm repeatedly. "We need to be untied when we strike!" he added, lifting his hand and unclenching his fingers. He spread his fingers and showed his open hand to all afore closing it into a tight fist before his eyes. "We mustn't poke them with one finger and then the next, but strike a full blow with our clenched fists!" He flung his fists wildly in the air, attracting many approving nods.

Men turned to one another with raised lips and nodded. Perhaps the colonel had something there, they mused. One could see it in their eyes, the colonel's words and flamboyant gestures had won them back from the edge of rashness, for the moment. I, for one, felt the tense air lift. He had done it. He had kept the lid from boiling over on top of the pot of anxious souls crowded in Forty Fort, and I tell you it was a fixin' to boil full over. Sound reason had somehow prevailed and lowered the flames of passion. I still admire him for that impossible task to this day. He was a good man.

Denison, realizing he had calmed the winds of war for but a moment, wasted no time in gathering his officers to him for a council of war. Action, even just the hint of it, would curb the beast writhing in people's souls. He had to keep them busy and occupied, therefore easing their minds. One had to think to worry.

He quickly assigned this one to this task and that one to another task. He put us boys to gathering green corn from the fields outside the gate, under the watchful eyes many a sentry, of course. I remember thinking how strange it was at the time, and of all things, hoping it would not come down to us having to eat green corn in fear of the runs that would surely ensue. Hundreds of people with the runs in that crowded fort would have been something, indeed. Something I wish not to recollect upon, but in hindsight would have gladly endured in the face of what happened next. Gladly, I tell you. Most gladly.

Chapter Fourteen

There are those dark moments which descend over mankind, which in themselves may not be the true test of endurance; but rather how one rises from the darkness, even if it is lit by the fires of destruction, and creates a new day. It is the true measure of man, and the nations he creates.

Such were the tests facing us huddled settlers in that fort long ago. Surrounded by nothing but the harsh and unforgiving wilderness, and with only ourselves to turn to for succor, we stood fast and faced the demons of war, urged on by the convictions which infuriated our foes in the first place. Liberty, I tell you, lived in each person's soul, young and old, and here we faced the truest test, for those fleeting of heart, or convictions, left long ago or deserted to the other side. This true test of ours was not ours alone, but a test of the convictions and principles of our new nation, and I am glad liberty did prevail in the end. But such we did not know at the time. We had not the luxury of hindsight. We had only those convictions and faith that what we were doing was right, not only for ourselves, but for our posterity. For let me tell you,

you, our posterity, were very much on our minds in those uncertain and troubled times, and I can only hope through these pages to reignite the flames of liberty born from our ancestors hearts, of which we were all born. Let us never forget them, or we shall forget a part of ourselves. A part which overcame impossible odds once, and with the resolve born of it, we may face and overcome any future such tests, and this nation shall forever live. For nothing can stand in its face. Not even defeat, for great things sometimes arise from ashes, priceless things, which stand the test of time. Such is Wyoming. When you look upon its beautiful mountains and vales, remember the ashes lying forever beneath its soil, for they had as much to do with everything gracing the valley today as the builder's hands whom made them.

It is in this light I continue this narrative, and hope that the struggles we all endured may never be forgotten, but live as a reminder of the greatness of this nation, this people, we Americans. May we never lose faith, and never let the light born from the passionate fires of liberty be extinguished by the gruff hands of tyrants, and forever liberty, and America, will shine in men's souls.

A shinning light did shine in most people's eyes, even in jittery Dan Washburn's eyes standing atop the platform over the gate at Forty Fort that faithful July morning. We boys rose before the light of dawn again, eager to witness the burgeoning promise of adventure. But the atmosphere definitely changed overnight. Dan barely turned his eyes from over the walls to recognize us, and only turned to confront us when one of the young Gore boys put his foot to the first rung of the ladder leading up to the platform. Dan turned around as smart as any soldier and pointed that big bayonet at the end of that long musket of his right down the ladder. We all blanched, to say the least, and stood shocked, nonetheless more than that poor Gore boy.

"You boys get!" he shouted. "We'll have none of your foolishness this day! And like I said afore, stay out from underfoot, for something is sure to happen this day, I'll grant you that fer sure!" With that he turned smartly about and stared over the wall again. All of the sudden he stopped shaking. He looked all the part of a soldier. His metamorphosis shocked us all. It was as if he grew into a man from a boy right afore our shocked eyes.

We all slowly turned and started walking away, looking back at that locked gate with a new feeling of apprehension. What did Dan see over that wall to change him so? Was the mere threat of war enough to change a man's demeanor?

We walked silent, all of our heads bowed in thought, when young Gore suddenly spoke. "The knot-hole!" he exclaimed. "Remember it! Just by first cabin over there! We can see out it, we can fer sure!"

All of us boy's eyes lit up and we all scrambled towards the cabin at the corner of the north wall. It seemed a race to see who would get there first and some of the bigger boys won. They hogged the slight knot hole in the wall some fool had etched out for who knows what reason, and pushed at one another to gain the rights to look out it. I am not one to cast dispersions, especially after all these years, but as a young one I can't recall just whose cabin sit next to the knot-hole. You see Forty Fort wasn't your average run of the mill fort, no sir, it had high walls, double thick, of hewed logs at that, and whoever found that knot hole on the inside had to carve through the outer log to get a hole clear through. As for what, as I said, I'll never know, for it was hard to tell Patriot from Tory sometimes, for some people are so deceptive, but I fear it was for no good. No good at all. Butler did have eyes about, for Captain Hewitt had captured two Indians spying on Forty Fort just a week afore the battle, Black Henry was one of them, and let me tell you I have never seen such cold steely eyes in all my born days. We hadn't been able to get a word out of neither of them though, even though John Franklin took a pair of bullet-molders to their fingers to get their tongues loosened a bit. It did not good, no how, for all we got was grins and that cold stare. Anyways, back to the knot-hole, it was just big enough for someone to pass something through as big as a grown-up's hand and it does cause some wonder of why it was there now, but then the exuberance of youth forsook such thoughts, we just wanted to see.

The noises of folks rising all around sounded behind us, but we ignored them. We knew the real show would happen right in front of this wall, Dan's wide eyes told us so. We all demanded at the same time for the boy occupying the hole to tell us what he saw. "Nothing! Nothing!" rang back to us time and time again afore young Gore finally forced his way through the bigger boys to catch a glimpse through the hole. His eyes grew wider than Dan's as the bigger boys gruffly grabbed him and forced him back to us smaller boys.

"What!?!" we asked all at once. "What'd ya see?"

The Gore boy's jaw dropped all the wider and he tore off towards his family's cabin without a word. We stood staring at one another and turned towards the older boys crowding around the hole. They remained silent, much to our despair. Their unearthly silence spooked us all.

A loud call of "Alarm! Alarm!" from the wall above made all us younger boys nearly jump out of our skin. All of the older boys immediately scattered and us younger boys scrambled to the hole, all of us peering through it at once, as we were much smaller.

There they stood across the field. All of the visions of our overactive imaginations faded in the face of reality. There they stood, one painted all up from head to foot with a single feather dancing in the breeze atop his skull cap, and the other in that hated green uniform we had heard so much about but never witnessed afore, until now. They looked as tall as the mountains and meaner than any of the beasts of the forest. There they were, the despoilers of all we knew. Those whom would trample our fields, burn our homes, and lay waste to all we had ever known as young folk. How I wished for Pa in that moment. Where are ya Pa? Off fighting some far away enemy while he truly marched to your own front door when you were away. Such horror, they represented to us, such gloom.

Suddenly absolute fear overtook us and none of us could move if we wanted, for here the demons of our imagination marched, right at us, out of our nightmares and into the light of day. Only a gruff hand yanking at us from behind pulled us from the hole. We all stood back with our jaw's agape, staring blankly up at the soldier hovering over us.

"Come now!" his booming voice exclaimed. Following our gaunt eyes, he bent down to the hole. "Here! What's this all about? Who did this? Was it you boys?"

All of us shook our heads and backed away.

The soldier cursed and answered his sergeant's call to man the walls. Giving us no more than a passing glance, he gruffly pushed us aside and headed towards the ladder. Many other men clamored around him, each anxiously waiting for his turn on the ladder. Up they went, one after another, with canteens clanging and muskets gripped tight in their white-knuckled fists.

We gawked at them for a few moments but then all the sudden rushed back to the hole. All of us scrunched our heads to the hole at the same time, squishing and scrunching our faces together until all had a glimpse of the advancing devils. We listened to the hubbub behind us but never turned to it, for we all settled into tight spots and if one moved he would sure lose his spot. Footsteps sounded behind us, advancing in a group which finally stopped at the gate. The loud creak of the door quickly opening and closing cocked all our heads as we craned to see just who stepped out to meet the devils. Colonel Denison, no doubt, but who joined him caused us all anxious moments.

"Bet ya it's John Franklin," somebody said.

"Naw, it ain't him, he ain't even about!" another answered.

"Lazarus!?!" all of us said at once, all thinking it only

fitting that our hero, the bravest man we knew, should certainly have the honor.

"Naw, they'd be shot by now, if'n he was here," a sane voice reasoned.

We had to silently agree and still sit tight with our faces all together, craning to look out the hole.

The Tory and Indian suddenly stopped and raised their eyes towards our advancing party. The man between them, dressed no plainer than any one else about Wyoming, seemed out of place. And another thing, he held no rifle as the other two.

"Why that there is Dan Ingersoll!" a voice said.

"It is!" we all agreed. A new thrill shot through our veins. Dan lived about Exeter and Fort Jenkins. If he lived, perhaps Johnny Jenkins did, also. I, for one, held my breath and gasped as the men from our fort strode into view.

"Johnny!" I said, recognizing him. "He made it! Must've come in this morning!" The other two men were no surprise, one being Colonel Denison and the other finely dressed man was unmistakably Lieutenant Colonel Dorrance.

We all watched silently and breathlessly as the men stood face to face talking. Though we couldn't hear across the distance, we watched each of their movements like a hawk. Johnny stood stoically, folding his arms across his chest. His head moved now and then, no doubt sizing up the enemy. Denison did most of the talking while Dorrance stood with one arm folded and his other hand cocked on his chin. He seemed to be also sizing up the enemy.

Strangely, Dan Ingersoll did most of the talking. He talked with his eyes staring down to the ground, in deep shame, and only raised them a few times. The green-coated Tory watched his every move, seeming to carefully gauge each of his words. He watched him with a stern, mean eye, one or two times raising his fist threateningly at poor Dan Ingersoll. He sure looked downcast and crestfallen, even at a distance, as if he had lost all the world. The painted Indian seemed to ignore his companions. His cold eye seemed to be sizing up our people. The solid look of hatred in his eyes shone across the distance, penetrating us boy's souls. Man, those people had a mean air about them. There was no question what they thought of someone. They did not wear their hearts on their sleeves in the least. If they loved you it showed, and if they hated you it showed, with no in-between. They could sure send chills right down a man's spine, that they could fer sure. The perfect bullies.

Finally old Dan Ingersoll must've touched the wrong nerve on that Tory fella for he right out smacked him hard on the back. Johnny Jenkins took a step forwards only to be countered by the painted Indian. We all stood breathless for a moment afore Colonel Denison raised a hand to calm the tense situation. A lot of movement showed in the far tree line beyond, no doubt many of the Tories and Indians lay in wait, watching the parley with equally intense eyes.

All the sudden the Tory waved his hands, seeming to be fit to be tied. He then pointed unmistakably at Johnny and raised his fists to the heavens in anger. We heard many rifle locks click along the wall in response.

Colonel Denison waved his hands equally as stern and captured the cold Tory's and Indian's eyes again. He made a few frustrated gestures of his own and waved a hand to the rifles and muskets bristling along the tall walls of Forty Fort behind him.

The Tory and Indian looked up and waved a hand behind them to the tree line.

All the men stood silent for an awful moment, each staring with eyes of pure hatred at one another. Poor Dan stood amidst it all, with the look of a man caught between this world and the next. He raised his bound hands up for all to see afore the Tory grabbed his hands and pulled them down, screaming something to the effect he had best behave or suffer the consequences latter. He finally did calm down and stare glumly down at the ground again.

Denison noticeably shook his head and spouted off a few curses afore turning smartly about and leading the others back to the gate.

The Tory glared at their backs for an awful long moment before his eyes rose to the rifles bristling along the walls again. The Indian shrugged his shoulders and turned about, walking leisurely towards the tree line. The Tory yelled a few expletives at the retreating Yankees and turned away in frustration, gruffly yanking poor Dan along behind him by a tether tied about his neck. I still feel for that poor man caught between the lines and used in such a cruel fashion. That Indian Butler could be a cruel man, as we were to find out shortly. Why he didn't march out to demand the surrender of the valley still befuddles me to this day. Could the heart of a coward beat in the chest of the Tory leader?

Men already scrambled out the south gate with the urgent call for war afore Colonel Denison and his party stepped back through the north gate. Denison immediately waved off the throngs of nervous men and women clamoring all about him and called for a runner to fetch Colonel Butler from Wilkes-Barre Fort at once! He then raised his hands and yelled to all, "we'll gather our forces and then figure out what to do! In the meantime keep a sharp eye and a clear head, for that is what we shall require the most of this day! Stay calm! We have a strong fort and I believe Indian Butler has no cannon! We can hold indefinitely!"

The immediate grumbles sounding from most people did little to effect the colonel's stance. He rubbed the back of his head and climbed the ladder to the platform above the gate, there to join the other anxious eyes staring into the deep forest beyond.

We boys stayed out from under foot but watched it all, and ran from one ruckus to another. Most of it occurred around the rum barrel. Men felt the need for a tonic to ease their souls in such times. It was thought rum let the thoughts flow through a man's mind as they flew from his tongue.

Chapter Fifteen

We swarmed around him as soon as he entered the gate, all blustering and pronouncing the need to march immediately out to meet the threat. There he was, Lazarus Stewart, the man, our hero of Wyoming, spouting words full of spirit, in spite of any threat. Oh, how youth can be infatuated by such boisterous men. I know, and tell you Lazarus Stewart a standing tall, with his glaring blue eyes shining out from under his wide-brimmed hat, embodied that spirit full, foolhardy or not. For what hero, or act of bravery, does not walk the fine line between foolhardiness and valor? For the foolish man does possess courage equal to the brave man. But if we were not all brave, each and every soul about Wyoming, we would not be here in the first place. Some just shine more than others, and speak louder. Such was buckskin-clad and tall Lazarus Stewart, Indian slayer, leader, and patriot.

We followed him, swaggering and jostling through the fort, yelling and carrying on, but we always noticed that admiring look out of the corner of his eye down to us. It meant more to us than anything else in the day. Our hero acknowledged us. We relished the thought!

Our hero soon drew more attention to himself than to the council of war assembling in front of the Bennett cabin. None of the eyes of the high officers turning to him glared more than Colonel Butler, on leave from the army, and ordered by General Washington himself to stay about Wyoming in the present crisis. He always wore a foreboding and sour look when he looked to Lazarus, his face expressing the question haunting his soul, what hath I brought to Wyoming? For it was he whom searched out the Paxtang Boys in our late troubles with the Pennamites and brought them here in 1770, well before my time, so I only know of the legends after the fact. As soon as the Paxtang Rangers, as they called themselves, arrived in the dead of winter, while Wyoming was in the throes of one of its struggles with the Penn's, they acted, taking the Pennamite Fort and creating mayhem which in turn would drive the Pennamites out of the valley. Loud and foreboding, they swore their undying allegiance to Wyoming, and since then had lived with us in their own section of the valley, they themselves christened Hanover Township. Captain Butler brought them there, and now had to put up with their oaths, among them, the only good Indian was a dead one, as well and the only way to fix a Tory was to stretch his neck! Such were our heroes. They had their opinions on matters, and to them that was the only one which mattered. I am glad to say my Uncle Rufus stood in their company, as full and proud as any of them. And if Pa could have wrangled his way out of General Washington's Life Guard as Uncle Rufus somehow did, he would have been standing tall in their ranks, too.

Lazarus, as every other Wyoming man at such gatherings in the fort, gravitated towards the rum barrels, carrying all his admirers with him. He stood aghast when one of the disgruntled men told him of Denison's earlier order to dump all of the rum stores, save one barrel for medicinal purposes, into the river.

"What balderdash!" Stewart immediately screamed. "Wasting good rum on the fish!?! I knew not their spirits were in so dire need of such uplifting spirits! Do we have poltroons at our lead!?! Rum is for men, not fishes!"

With that, he turned and marched towards the council of war, waving his hands in the air in frustration. Many followed whom before had been waiting in the shadows, perhaps for such light Lazarus now bore.

Denison and Butler both rolled their eyes and initially turned their backs to him, feigning ignorance of his presence. In no time Lazarus' bombastic voice boomed louder than all the rest, reluctantly turning the officers of the council of war towards him.

Denison immediately pointed his finger towards his friend. "Dear Lazarus," he said, "I ask you to refrain from such boisterous acts whilst we discuss the matters at hand in this council."

95

Lazarus' cold eyes darted directly towards him. He rubbed his chin and shook his head. Perhaps his friendship with Denison held him at bay, but even friendship fails in the face of a man so possessed with such great opinions.

All eyes watched our silent hero for his response, but still he stood silent, anxiously tapping his foot of the ground. Even in moccasins the force of his infuriated foot tapping on the ground sounded loud in the still air. He drew a deep breath and prepared to speak when Butler strode to the front waving his hands away from the cabin. "A private soldiers' place is not about here, this is a meeting of officers," he said, cocksure and proud. "I ask that you give way sir, as we may proceed."

Everyone gasped.

"Proceed in what, fine sir?" Lazarus asked.

"Discussing the matter now distressing us all, of course," Butler said.

"Discuss hell!" Lazarus boomed. Butler had opened the door for him, and he intended to stride through it. He immediately straightened his back and strode up to the haughty officer. "As every man here has a stake in such decisions, I say he shall have a say in them!"

A great resounding huzza echoed through the fort. Butler blanched in the face of it all.

"No, no," Denison said, stepping between the two men. He put his hand to Lazarus' shoulder and whispered something in his ear. He then stepped back and declared, "we are only discussing the disposition of our troops and such. We must obtain a proper count of our enemy's forces! Level heads are what's needed!"

"Well, you'll not find leveler heads than atop you square headed bastards!" a voice boomed in response.

Lazarus', and all eyes, turned in the direction of the voice. Lazarus rubbed his chin and looked deathly into his friend's eyes. Perhaps things had spiraled out of control a bit.

"Need I remind you, dear friend," Denison said, "the enemy is out there, not in here."

Lazarus bit his lip and shook his head all the more. "A poltroon is every sensible man's enemy, no matter the rank!" he said through gritted teeth.

A chorus of outraged voices sounded in response, some in defense of the colonels, some sharing Lazarus' view on matters. We New England people did, and still do, believe every man should have a voice in the matters that effect his life. It is just our way, what with our traditions of town meetings and such. I still believe it to be the best way, in spite of what happened that day. Such are the costs of freedom. Nothing is perfect, not man nor beast, the whole world wide. A man should be the captain of his own fate.

A rather heated argument ensued, with folks divided on one side or the other. It lasted well into the afternoon hours. At first the officers sided with the colonels, but with the reports of newly arriving scouts stating they felt the enemy's numbers no greater than their own, the colonels' argument that they all remain in the fort and await the other companies scrambling to the fort fell mute. I must say, eyes glared and eyes bulged, with fingers pointing threateningly at many faces. The intensity of it all even hushed us children, watching our elders argue with such forceful gestures and all. Tensions did run high. These men held unshakable beliefs, none the more than each man had a say in his own fate. As I said, such are the costs of a free society. I, myself, still stand behind it, and all of those brave men, no matter what side they held on the matter.

Heated tongues continued throwing stinging accusations of foolhardiness and cowardice when someone rolled forth the 'medicinal' barrel of rum and cracked open its head. Noggins, buckets, gourds, and canteens, immediately sank into it, soon bringing things to head, to say the least. By this time it is safe to say a rather strained friendship, if any all, remained between Denison and Stewart. Such was that war, it tore families asunder, and destroyed countless friendships.

Finally Lazarus' sharp tongue convinced most of the officers their duty lay beyond the walls, not within them, especially when scouts reported some outlying farms being put to the torch. Stewart's argument of just what was this military force assembled for but to prevent such actions rang true to many of their hearts.

Soon the frustrated colonels' had no choice. With the loudest voice I heard that day Denison announced their intent to march out and meet the hated enemy, come hell or high water. Resounding cheers and fists full of mugs, canteens, gourds, and noggins rose in agreement. Butler added he would lead, if they dared follow!

Wyoming had made up it's mind. The collective had decided for the whole, right or wrong. Simple courage demanded no other action.

The new American colors-adopted and established but a year before-rose in the hands and over the heads of those true patriots. Fifers immediately squealed at the head of the forming ranks and the thud of the drum quickly joined them. The lively air of St. Patrick's Day in the Morning hastened many steps and soon the column of patriots marched lively out of the north gate, with all of us left in the fort tagging along and cheering that grand new flag and the brave patriots under it. It was a stirring site indeed, and my heart still flutters when I see it in my mind's eye, even after all these years. All seemed certain of our cause and our actions. Somehow we felt under these footsteps marched the faith and promise of the future nation. The ground seemed to reverberate with its promise.

Us boys stopped cheering as the column disappeared up the road and looked to the skeleton of a man also watching them. Johnny's eye bore the expectant look of a young boy left behind while his father went hunting, as if he anxiously waited for a yell back from the ranks for him to join them. But alas, he knew himself too weak from the rigors of captivity he had endured at the hands of our enemies. Weak in body, he remained stout of heart, and no doubt would do his best as commandant of the fort in the colonel's absence. Duty, that sense which binds an honorable man to his tasks, also shone from his eyes. I felt proud of Johnny just then, and felt proud he called all in my family friend. By the look in the other boys' eyes shining up at Johnny, I knew they felt the same about the stalwart man. He proved a good example of a man.

Another young boy, barely a teenager himself, broke our admiring stares up at Johnny. He clamored up to Johnny just a eying the rifle he held loosely in his hands.

Johnny's eyes fell to the anxious boy and afore he could open his mouth the boy snatched his rifle from his hands and rushed after the column.

Stunned, Johnny took a few fruitless steps after the running boy before raising his hands in frustration and yelling, "Stop! Jabez! Stop!"

We boys watched with wonder, envious of Jabez for his age, and courage.

"Can't Johnny!" Jabez yelled back over his shoulder. "I just gotta go and catch up with Joseph and Paw! Can't miss out of this! I just can't!"

Johnny's shoulders fell and he bowed his shaking head. Turning, his eyes glared at the man standing and facing him. He too shared the same look Jabez bore but a few moments afore.

"The boy's right Johnny," the old man said. "My bones may be a bit old, but my soul's as young as the next. I got to go too, I hope you understand." With that he bowed his head, adverting his eyes from Johnny's questioning stare.

"George Cooper," he called behind the man, "we do need men about this fort in case things go astray, God forbid."

"Oh, they'll be going astray alright, by for the Tories!" George answered over his shoulder. "That's why I got to go, got to see to dear Cherrick, got to keep him from mischief, wouldn't feel right if something was to happen to him, nor any of the others."

Johnny took off his hat and ran frustrated hand through his hair. He looked to the man by the gate and waved his hand to him to close the gate, he himself giving him a hand.

"We can't all be in the ball," he said. "Someone's got to mind the door."

A ruckus at the south gate turned us all around. We all rushed towards the commotion, craning our heads around the gathering grown-ups to see. Breaking through the crowd with the advantage of being small and fleet of foot, we all gasped at the exhausted column of mounted men reining up their lathered mounts in front of us all.

"Dear God," the exhausted man in the lead of the small column gasped, "food, we need food, we have not broken our fast this day!"

Women immediately scrambled to their kitchens. Every eye of Johnny's old men and boys manning the walls stared down in wonder of the men.

Johnny strode through the crowd, suddenly invigorated and robust. He gathered the reins of the lead man's exhausted horse and looked up to the man. "My God, Pierce, it's good to see you!" he exclaimed, craning his head to look behind the five mounted men. "Where is Spalding and the rest? Are they afoot behind you?"

"Yes," Pierce mumbled, "but much further than you think, much further, some thirty some miles, I reckon." He promptly plopped down from his horse and eagerly grabbed some of the biscuits the returning women offered him. He took a few quick bites and craned his own neck around the wide eyed skeleton of a man standing before him. "My God Jenkins," he gasped, "what has happen to you?"

"The hole at Niagara," Johnny said, crestfallen.

"Where's Colonel Denison?" Pierce quickly asked. "I must report!"

"They've marched to meet Indian Butler, they have, just left in fact," Johnny answered.

Pierce's eyes lit up, as well as all the other men's eyes. The rest of the men quickly dismounted and gathered their pouches and such from their exhausted and lathered horses. They all neighed in relief, seeming as so a quick gust of wind would knock them over to the ground. Their knees even shook.

"These horses is played out," Pierce said through bites of biscuit, "we must go afoot, and at the long trot boys!"

Without even a nod to Johnny they all scrambled through the crowd towards the north gate, yelling for it to be opened in their haste. They all gathered handfuls of biscuits and took quick gulps of rum handed to them as they passed.

Only one, a colored man named Gershom Prince, stopped for but a second in front of Johnny. "Captain Durkee?" he gasped between bites of biscuit.

"He's fine, last I seen him," Johnny answered, nodding to the north gate. "He's up there, at the head of the column, as he should be."

"Much obliged," Gershom said with his own nod. He quickly scampered off behind his fellows.

I still find it strange how a man in bondage could feel so for his master, even after all these years. Though the peculiar institution is still in practice in certain parts of this country, through a slow and arduous process it has been abolished in this part of the country. I shuddered to think what it may cost this nation to abolish it as a whole. Perhaps, I fear, only blood shall cleanse this land.

Wyoming had a few people in bondage in those days, though I must admit it was seen as the ultimate hypocrisy by most men whom professed freedom so vehemently. I still remember the black codes and sundown laws of Connecticut, of which Wyoming was a part of then. I well remember Elizabeth, the Slocum's servant, and Lisburn, Colonel Butler's man. In my youth, when these upper lands of Wyoming were being settled, I well remember seeing and hearing tell of Ezra Spalding's old black woman in Minnequa, or present Canton.

And of course, dear Quocko, whom died for liberty, and his friend Gershom, whom now, though emancipated, marched out to meet another threat to freedom, the King.

Perhaps freedom has to be won one step at a time.

Chapter Sixteen

We watched the rushed men of Captain Spalding, five in all, dart through the north gate amongst many cheers which quickly subdued when the gate creaked closed. I, for one, felt a great lump growing in my throat, and feared I couldn't speak past if I wanted. But I did not want to. Such a strange mingled feeling I never wish to endure again, a feeling of hope shadowed by fear.

All of us boys just glanced at one another until the Gore boy cocked his head towards the knot-hole. We all suddenly felt drained and unsure, with a sudden desire to visit another part of the fort.

We all rambled along in the suddenly quiet fort to the stockade, there to peek into the face of the miscreants we already held for an answer to it all. Who were our men to face? Were they really as cruel as legend said? These questions nagged at our souls. We answered them by peeking through the cracks in the door holding our enemies.

Stark eyes immediately darted to us. We jumped in spite of ourselves, no exactly sure how the demon's eyes caught sight of us in the first place, for we had moved so silently. Slowly we eased back to the door and stared back at those piercing dark eyes staring at us from the shadows. They bore no hint of mercy, but only a fierce resolve. Absolute hatred seemed to embody them. We turned away from the one Indian sitting cross-legged on the floor before us to the other scrunched all in a ball in a dark corner. He seemed not to share Black Henry's absolute hatred, but only sat perfectly still, with his knees all curled tight up to his chest. The fleeting glimpse he did cast to us bore no animosity, but only the hollow look of the forlorn, as if he wished to be anywhere but in his present predicament. Oh, but Black Henry's eyes glared enough for both of them, as a caged beast whom hungered for blood and would slash and kill in an instant if free. It brought us no succor, but fear. Oh God be with our brave men, I silently prayed, for they shall need you today. I suddenly thought of

Grandpa up there on the walls with Hooker Smith and the rest of his *Reformadoes,* as the aged men of the Alarm List company called themselves. Too old, or young, to march out on the field proper, they proved best for garrison duty, and guarding prisoners. All of the sudden I wished to be near him, if for nothing else, but to be around family.

I eased back from the door and scrambled along the wall, instantly followed by a train of other boys. Seeming lost on what to do in such a suddenly alien atmosphere, they emptily followed anyone with an idea on how to quell the growing feeling of angst in the tense and quiet air.

Spying Grandpa staring out over the wall up on the platform near the north gate, I flew up the ladder to his side, followed by the throng of boys.

Grandpa glanced down to us out of the corner of his eye, but mostly his eyes remained fixed to the north, intently searching the horizon. He didn't even speak to acknowledge us, but only shook his head. Perhaps the lump in his throat forbade him from speaking, too, I thought, easing up to look over the wall. Of course all of the boys followed my lead.

Nothing stirred beyond the walls but the wind blowing gently through the grass and leaves of the trees. It all seemed so peaceful and silent. Nature, forever turning, even in the waves man threw in her way. Nothing seemed to stop her flow through time. Our troubles suddenly seemed insignificant compared to the ceaseless flow of time, but then Grandpa muttered something, turning all our eyes to him.

He looked down to us and then to his musket. "They're up there, just beyond the trees," he said, louder this time. "There they'll meet the devil this day, to be freemen or dead, for I fear there will be no quarter given this day."

We all blanched in the face of Grandpa's glum words when all hell suddenly cracked in our ears, giving us all a start. The distant lone crack of a rifle sounded again. A great hush of expectancy blanketed the fort. Everyone stopped where they stood and listened. We boys all stared breathlessly over the pointed logs. What did it mean? The awful silence between shots seemed to last a lifetime. Then, one, two, three, and a dozen more cracks echoed down the river. It had begun!

Soon women climbed the ladders to the walls, ignoring the cold eyes of the boys and old men. They would hear come hell or high water, they said with their stern looks and wide eyes. All of Forty Fort's huddled settlers stopped and listened, with nary a whisper passing among anyone.

The dozens of shots grew into the distinct crack of an organized volley of musketry. All held their breaths. Sporadic cracks sounded in answer, but then another volley quickly silenced them. A third volley sounded, answered by a terrible combined shrill I still carry in my nightmares and every waking moment and fear I shall for all eternity.

The cascading yells echoed from far up the valley but somehow felt as near as my foot to my hand. We all quivered, listening to the frightening crescendo grow. True fear gripped us all, many fell to their knees and muttered unceasing prayers under their breaths. Doctors Gustin and Hooker Smith both noticeably blanched and went about hastily increasing the section of the fort laid out for their butchery, as some called it.

I myself have never felt a greater sense of sadness in all my born days. But I stared ahead, like the other boys, I found not the strength in my frozen body to turn away. The devils had struck our men, our fathers, our brothers, our uncles, friends, and grandfathers. No longer did their trained and organized volleys fill the air, but the strange howling, desperate, and mingled roar of men in great combat. A noise, once you hear, you shall never forget, at any distance, or time. My imagination gripped me in its awful throes, flashing visions of this friend and that friend falling valiantly to a merciless foe. Oh dear God, I muttered on trembling lips, please let them live, please let them live.

My prayer drew my Grandfather's eyes down to me. His wide eyes offered no answer, but only a shared shock. "It does not sound good," he muttered. "It does not sound good.

You best see to yer Ma and Grandma."

I had only to turn and look down to see them both hovering below the platform below us, both of them pacing back and forth with their hands cupped to their mouths as if to hold in their cries. Many other women did the same thing all around the fort, some collapsing on the platforms.

"Here! See to them," Johnny's voice sounded so near it made us all jump. "Somehow it broke the horror of the distant sounds. Somehow it brought us back into the light of day.

"See to these women folk," he ordered his men, waving his hands to and fro. "We must all be strong! We need good and just men now more than ever! Keep to your posts and stand strong. We have the walls, do not forget, we have strong walls."

His last words did little to encourage the failing women and now most of them openly burst into tears. Cries and wails sounded all through the fort, mixing with the awful tell-tale noises creeping into the fort, and into our souls. Oh dear God, help us. Such a chill I have never felt before ran down my spine.

"Get down to yer Ma, now, Moses and Will!" Grandpa ordered. "And that goes fer the rest of ya too!"

I looked up to Grandpa with my hollow eyes but suddenly lost the will to move my feet. "What will become of us?" I muttered. "What'll they do to us Grandpa?"

"Nothing, if'n I has any say in it!" Grandpa blurted out, shuffling me along with his boot. "Now get out from under foot and behave, for you can hear, can't you? The devils may be soon at this gate!"

Tears started rolling uncontrollably down my cheeks. All the boys started crying something fierce, but dutifully obeyed and scampered back down the ladder. Our Ma's met us all and ushered us close. Some collapsed, holding one another in a great hug, while others shooed their young ones to the cabins. All wore that awful look. That hollow look of uncertainty. Tears wetted each cheek all the more as the horrible sounds echoed through the fort.

The low muffled sounds of distant musketry mingled with savage yells started to be punctuated by excruciating cries of pain and terror. Cries which seemed to grow closer, drawing everyone back up to the walls. They soon lined the entire wall, despite the protests of the *Reformadoes*. Every eye stared towards the approaching sounds of horror, still somehow clinging to a fleeting sense of hope. Silent and still they stood.

Johnny rushed down a ladder to the gate, sending two exhausted scouts from the night before up the road to scout the ridge. He himself stumbled a few rods in front of the gate, his pistols raised in expectation. The strong thud of madly approaching hooves perked his, as well as everyone else's, head up.

The scouts backed down over the ridge from the road, seeming shocked. A horse thudded between them, its rider sagging in the saddle and yelling a jumbled warning at the top of his lungs, his tongue twisted with the terror shining in his eyes.

Women gasped all along the walls, most rushing up to the north gate. The platform creaked under the weight of the sudden rush.

Johnny stood aghast, backing up to the gate and yelling to the mad rider. He raised his hands to stop the terrified rider and mount but stood back, noticing the odd angle of the man's bleeding right leg in a stirrup.

The gate flew open and the man rode through into the awaiting throngs rambling down from the walls. "What has happen to our brave men!?!" echoed from a hundred anxious throats to the man. "What? Pray tell us, what has happen!?!"

A lone word sounded from the man's trembling lips as he collapsed to the ground. A word which started panic, massacre! Massacre!

A dozen more men soon struggled past the two scouts, some falling into ditches along the road from exhaustion and loss of blood before the overwhelmed men. All but a few showed weaponless and terrified. All their eyes bulged with fear and absolute disbelief. Every man showed bloody. Some tumbled through the gate to hundreds of pleading eyes and probing hands, all grabbing them to recognize them through the gaunt look of absolute terror strongly distorting their faces. The poor men seemed to be passed along the line of women until fortunately recognized by family or friends. All rambled incoherently about the massacre! Massacre!

Women flooded the gate, pouring out to meet the fugitives stumbling to the fort from the north. One after another the wounded and dispirited men tumbled to them, all under Johnny's increasingly anxious eyes.

"Doctors! Doctors!" he screamed to an overwhelmed Hooker Smith and Doctor Gustin already scrambling from one wounded man to the next. They started directing the shocked women to place this one here and that one there. "My God! My God! What are we to do?" many gasped.

"First get them all back inside the fort, man!" Hooker Smith yelled. "For all of hell has touched these men, and it'll soon sting us fer sure!"

"You're right! You're right!" Johnny yelled, suddenly regaining his composure after the first shock of the totally defeated men. "Every able man to the walls!" he yelled to the confused masses. "Women inside the gate, hold it open but a sliver to receive these poor souls, and brace yourselves for the shock coming at their heals! Brace yourselves and fire sure, but only if ye be sure of yer shot!"

Women flooded back through the gate and the poor exposed scouts stood manfully to their posts just over the ridge, watching the men stumbling past them, none with more than an incoherent rant to answer their pleas. What horror descended on Wyoming? What horror descended upon America?

Through the groans and increasing wails of anguish

inside the fort distant yells still sounded, creating a confused, mingled, cacophony echoing from one wall to the other.

Bleary eyed men along the walls, their eyes clouded with age, tears, or the contagious horror shining from their fleeing brethren's eyes, stood with their muskets and rifles pointing over the walls. The overwhelmed pair of doctors, yelling instructions to this one and that one, ran from one poor wounded soul creeping through the gate to another, sweat clouding their eyes and drenching their clothes.

Us children, immediately enlisted to draw water, gather bandages, and help hold down quivering men wounded in the most horrible fashions, rose to the moment, with only the innocent infants escaping duty. Wyoming gathered strong to rise to the relief of their poor wounded soldiers, becoming lost in their duties, though tears ran down everyone's cheeks. It seemed an odd tonic, mixed with fear and misery, but it somehow soothed the panic.

With the veil of darkness slowly descending, first one crestfallen colonel rode through the gate atop a bloodied mount, and then a few moments later, the other. Both seemed totally shocked, but Butler appeared the worse, rambling on about his children, his children, stand fast my children! Even when his wife helped him down from his exhausted mount he kept rambling, despite her pleas. His eyes wore a strange thousand yard stare, as if his eyes looked at you, but through you, as if they had seen the great beyond this day and somehow remained on the edge of eternity between this world and the next.

Colonel Denison, though also noticeably shaken, seemed able to attend to his duties. Dismounting, he immediately rambled up the nearest ladder to the walls, staring intently out to that horrible battlefield beyond the trees and barking orders to Johnny and his men afore finally collapsing from exhaustion. Helped to the Bennett's cabin, his anxious wife finally calmed him, though Colonel Butler remained quite agitated and stunned for quite a while in the same cabin.

Chapter Seventeen

That horrible night passed into the welcoming light of day, much to our relief, for no one but the babes slept that night. The cries continued all night, each one scratching down our spines.

I prayed that night most heartily, as did all. I prayed for the poor wounded, my Pa, fighting somewhere out there with General Washington while his own family suffered so on his own home soil, and for myself and every frightened survivor. Those screams and yells in the night drowned out the doleful call of the whippoorwills, and the croak of the bullfrogs. Those distant drums echoing among the screams still sound in my heart to this day. Oh, and the poor women, exasperated and broken, some stumbling around in a mindless march all night mumbling, oh, my dear husband, what will become of us now, or other mournful cries. Some infants clung to their dresses all the night, catching a few winks when their mothers stopped their ceaseless pacing to gasp for a new breath. Tears poured from every eye, even the overworked doctors. Oh what a sight. Oh what a feeling.

I managed to scrunch in some dark corner, listening in horror as hell enfolded all around. I tell you there is no escaping hell, once you are in it you are in it, and my soul, though young, remembers each minute of that horrible night better than I remember yesterday. It forever lives, and haunts, my soul. That horrible night I gained no sleep or rest, but only a few winks, for that is all the living hell would allow.

Finally the sun crept over the walls, but I sat still, unable to move. What shall this day bring but throngs of victorious Indians? Looking up to the walls I knew the old men, young men, and few stout-hearted women manning the walls to be insignificant compared to the victorious hordes feasting and celebrating their victory all night, torturing and exacting their pound of flesh-Wyoming flesh. Now they would come to satisfy their bloodlust in full. Now our hair would be the price freedom would pay this day. Nothing could seem to stop them, not my brave Grandpa or Johnny. All seemed lost, but for one bloody half-naked soul trudging before me in my dark corner with Johnny at his heels in the early morning light.

The sight of the man brought one of the hovering women out of her trance and she promptly offered him an old blanket to cover him. Noticing the blood about his shoulder, she fussed about him under his shaking eye. "No need," he told her, "the shot went clean through, dear lady, attend to others who may be of greater need!"

The woman reluctantly turned away. Bowing her head, she seemed to be drawn back into her lethargic state by the long hand of mourning.

The man and Johnny continued on, discussing the grim state of affairs. I perked up. Drawn by the two stalwart men's courage, I rose from my corner and scampered behind them, eagerly listening to them.

"Barely thirty have returned from the field," Johnny said, "most of them are wounded, and all are of long hearts."

The man glanced around in the pale light, scanning all around with a long soulful look. "Yes, it is most distressing, but we must buck up, for the hell about that field may soon demand entrance to this fort, and," he said with a long pause, "they are giving no quarter, that I assure you."

Both of the men stopped and sat upon a bench, seeming overcome by the mere thought of the horrors to come.

"Ah, lad," the man said, noticing me hovering about them. "You Bennetts are a fine lot! Your dear Solomon gave me the shirt off his very back after I stumbled upon him near the river after I swam across for my dear life." He gazed down to his shoulder and winced. "Caught a ball, I did as I swam, had to strip down to the bone as I ran, but managed to save the last Guinea in me pocket!" He shook his head in disgust. "Put it in my mouth for the swim and lost it when one of the rat's balls caught my shoulder! A whole Guinea mind you!"

We both looked in wonder at the man, amazed by his concern for coin amidst this all, but then reconsidered, knowing the frugal storekeeper to be most mindful of coin.

"Such are the sufferings of war," Johnny said.

"Yes, most unfortunate," Mathias Hollenback said, suddenly straightening his back and standing. "Oh, the last man I saw on the field was our dear Captain Durkee, dreadfully wounded, but still the soldier, insisting that I leave him and make good my own escape." He paused for a moment and swallowed hard against the thought. "Brave to the last," he mumbled, straightening his back all the more. "I found a canoe and made my way back here, had too!" He stopped and suddenly looked down to his ragged blanket. "Have you any clothes for my person and a bit to eat? I must ride at once to hasten on Spalding and his relief forces!"

"Hadn't you best report?" Johnny asked, slowly rising. He stared blankly into Hollenback's eyes.

"You have told me all I need to know and I have told you everything I know!" Hollenback said. "Now are you to help, or am I to ride on alone?"

"I'll help," Jenkins said, gesturing towards a cabin.

They both disappeared into it for a few minutes afore Hollenback strode through the door, fully dressed and munching hastily on a biscuit. Another man, besides Johnny, soon followed. The new man immediately saddled two horses.

"Is not this Major Garrett's mount?" Hollenback asked, rubbing a hand over the blood-smeared horse. His shoulder seemed all the better, with a mere spot of blood marking his wound. The spirit healed the body quickly.

Johnny nodded, then shook his head.

Hollenback nodded back and quickly mounted. "I and Hageman here will ride for Spalding!" he loudly announced, reining his mount towards the south gate. Johnny and I trotted along them, with Johnny gesturing to the sentry at the gate to open it for the hard-riding men. The gate quickly opened and closed in their wake. The sound of their hard hooves upon the ground soon faded. Silence, with its gloom, quickly descended over the fort again.

Chapter Eighteen

Colonel Denison suddenly appeared from a cabin, rubbing his disheveled hair and staring about. His clean and fine hunting shirt seemed out of place with the haunted look on his face and his torn and dirty trousers. He marched up to Johnny standing hollow-eyed by the south gate. I ducked behind Johnny from his stern eyes.

"Who was that thundering about before dawn?" he asked Johnny.

"Hollenback, sir," Johnny said, looking as if he had lost something or missed a great opportunity. "He's riding for to hasten on Spalding."

A series of quick rifle shots from beyond the gate suddenly gave us all a start. The sentries on the wall immediately peered over the pointed logs. We all looked up to them, anxiously awaiting word. A pair of shaking heads answered our pleas. "We can see nothing, sir," one of them mumbled down to us in the silence.

More people rose from the rifle shots. Women immediately crowded around, all of them staring blankly at Johnny and Colonel Denison.

"It's nothing," Denison finally muttered. "Nothing, now go back and get your rest, for you may need it this day."

He took Johnny by the arm and scooted him near the gate, looking about with his darting eyes to keep everyone at bay. Both men spoke on hushed whispers before Johnny nodded his head profusely and backed away. His eyes suddenly darted around and locked on me, all staring at him in wonder.

Johnny's hollow eyes beamed to life. He stared at me for the longest moment, seeming to stare beyond me. His eyes glared with a new light, as if he suddenly saw his own unborn children represented in my presence. He turned his eyes towards Denison and removed his hat with all the dignity of the finest gentleman.

"I must ride for Captain Spalding, sir," he said.

Denison raised his eyebrows and the frowned. He rolled an eye to the poor souls manning the walls and shook his head. "Yes," he said, "you must do as you see fit."

Johnny needed no other word. He ran to the stables, saddled, mounted, and rode out the gate in more time than it takes to tell of it. In fact, he moved so fast I stood stunned by it all. A tired-eyed Will soon stood by my side, wiping his eyes. "Was that Johnny?" he asked. "Where's he a going?"

"To fetch help," I muttered down to him. "That's all."

A commotion towards the cabins turned us both about. There stood Colonel Butler, looking all regal and smart, but nonetheless still carrying that sad look about his face. He adverted his eyes from the many questioning eyes staring at him and waved a hand to Denison. Denison sauntered over to him, seeming painfully aware of the eyes watching them.

The reason of Colonel Butler's angst soon showed itself in the haunted face of Mrs. Butler. Cradling their babe close to her person, she also adverted her eyes from all the eyes cast in their direction. A young lad produced two fine horses from the stable to which he and Colonel Butler immediately loaded with goods, so much so the colonel himself had to strap and tie, of all things, a feather mattress, atop his saddle. He then helped his wife to the top of it and after handing their babe up to her, mounted himself, with a great helping hand from Colonel Denison and the lad.

The dozen or so Continental soldiers suddenly climbing down from the walls greatly heightened the concern in everyone's eyes to say the least. After a few hasty words with both colonels they promptly sped out the south gate, creating a great collective gasp in their wake. Colonel Butler himself waved a hand down to Denison and turned to the crowd, sitting tall atop the mattress and crowded horse's back. I swear the packhorse behind them appeared nothing but a set of legs sticking out of the bottom of a great bundle.

"Good people!" he said. "Do not be concerned! If the terms are just I am sure none of you shall be harmed, but I a m also quite certain, no matter how favorable the terms, such will not be the fate of I and the soldier's of the Line if captured! That is why we are departing to Wilkes-Barre Fort, there to await word of the terms. If need be our escape would prove better from there, as from here, so close to our foe!" With that he slowly snapped the reins in his hands and the overloaded horses trudged out of the south gate. Many settlers hastily gathered their things to follow, despite Denison's reassurances. The moment grew tense, slowly heightening to a very real panic.

A loud call from the north gate momentarily halted everything. "A man approaches!" echoed through the hushed crowd. Denison took advantage of it and immediately ordered the gates closed, no matter whom protested. He strode to the north gate, with the anxious crowd in tow.

Ma appeared out of nowhere and gathered us two boys close to her. Her eyes darted to and fro, up to the walls and then to the poor pitiful wounded being hovered over by the frenzied doctors under the platform a few yards away. Their pitiful moans haunted the air. As we stood huddled to Ma's dress the expectant crowd pushed us along with them. Will stayed clinging to Ma's dress, but I ran with the other boys to our secret window, the knot-hole.

We all crowded and scrunched together until all eyes caught a sliver of a glimpse through the knot-hole and all gasped. There he stood, all tall and bright as day in his green uniform, the scourge of Wyoming himself, Parshall Terry. Such a nerve, this man, of all our enemies. With him, it truly was a brother's war, and my heart still goes out to the poor patriotic Terry family huddled in the crowded fort with us. Oh, how their hearts must have burst! A definite hush rolled down the anxious eyes peering over the walls, along with the distinct click of dozens of firelocks being cocked and no doubt pointed right at the traitor's heart! Damn him!

They bantered on and on, both Denison and Terry, for what seemed the longest time. Oh, how the tones of a traitor do burn a patriot's ears! Apparently Colonel Denison found the need to buy time, even at his dignity's expense. No doubt he considered Butler's and the regular soldier's plight, and wished to gain more time for them to gain distance, and therefore safety.

Finally, with the pronouncement from the Tory's tongue that a surrender this day would save any innocents from going under the hatchet, all fell silent. I heard a creak above in the silence, apparently the words took Denison aback so much he pushed himself back from the wall. At this moment all of us boys never heard such cursing in our life, all along the wall and from an odd fellow standing near the gate. I turned an eye to see the man Jonathan Terry, the fiend's own brother, hastily load his rifle. He angrily pushed towards the gate, only to have more leveler headed sentries push him back, and warn him, not this day, but soon, young Terry. He shook his head with such force spittle flew from his foaming cheeks. Such anger. I had never afore seen a man so angry as to foam at the mouth. But let me tell you, they do, in certain situations. Terry fell to his knees and dropped his rifle in frustration. His clenched fists rose to his eyes and slammed them so I feared for him to knock himself senseless, but another man soon stopped him and escorted him away from the gate, and out of earshot.

Denison yelled something furiously back at the hated Tory, but quickly regained his composure. I heard him tell many to stand down as it would not do to kill the messenger, foul though he was. He bluntly agreed to a meeting at one of the clock in the afternoon and turned away from the wall, leaving the Tory glaring at the dozens of firelocks all aimed at his heart.

I swear I saw him flinch, for soon after streams of sweat poured down his face. He swallowed hard and backed carefully to the wood line, and his brethren. That walk must have seemed the longest in his life, for I sure didn't breathe in anticipation of the shot which was sure to ring out, but alas didn't, though the Tory would die latter in some mysterious circumstances back at Niagara by the Lake, the Tory settlement set up by the British for displaced men after the war. Justice, Wyoming justice, did bide its time, but did strike full, at least in those bygone days. One of the Tory Wintermoots was administered the same there abouts, too. Such is Wyoming justice.

No sooner than the Tory disappeared into the woods than another commotion tore us from the knot-hole. We turned and all ran towards the noise of clanging pots and fouls curses.

The York children scrambled into the kitchen, each emerging with a hasty bundle and wide-eyes. Mrs. York quickly stomped behind them, raising her spoon high in the air and screaming bloody murder. "No!" she screamed to the eyes staring at her, "I'll have none of it, nor should any of you! He's the foulest of the foulest, that rat is! He deprived me of a husband and my dear children a father! And he'll administer the same to ye all! That I'll grant ye fer sure!"

She stopped and waved her spoon all around. Suddenly locking her eyes onto it, she cast it away, her way of resigning her position. She ground it into the ground with her foot and spat, nodding her head to all around. She then waved her children towards the south gate and stomped to it, confronting the exhausted old man standing by the gate.

"Here now," the old fellow said, twirling around to confront the storming woman and her brood. "Colonel Denison said none is to leave this gate, and that's the way of it! So back off!" The old man's tired eyes betrayed no mercy. His exhausted body could offer nothing but blind obedience to the letter of his orders. Thinking became lost in his exhausted haze.

Mrs. York would have none of it, she stomped headlong towards the gate, only stopping by the point of the old man's bayonet shaking nervously in his hands. "Are you to open that gate!?!" she sternly asked.

"No ma'am," the sentry said, "duty forbids it!" His eyes widened to the sight of Colonel Denison himself marching towards the gate.

"Here Mrs. York!" Denison screamed. "Come now! What are you about? Have we not enough troubles?"

"Troubles!" Mrs. York screamed back, "that's just what you yourself have invited into these very walls! Your misplaced trust is not shared by me! I'll not stay here to have that Tory bastard destroy what remains of my family! No sir!" she added, turning to glare at the sentry. "You'll have to run me through!"

Unbelievably, she pushed her body forwards, forcing the butt of the old sentry's shaking musket against the gate.

The old man's eyes bulged, but he stood fast in his impossible predicament. He knew not what else to do, or where to turn, but to stunned Colonel Denison.

Denison stepped closer and blanched at the sight of the trickle of blood showing on her dress at the point of the pressing bayonet. She meant every word she said, indeed.

Denison scratched his head and looked down to the children. "I'll not have these innocents' blood on my hands, you must desist in this outrageous behavior, Mrs. York, please!"

Mrs. York only glared back at him. She pushed her body even harder against the bayonet.

The sentry gasped in amazement. War had driven this woman insane! he thought, but still stood fast.

Denison looked to the stunned eyes all around him, and to the gathering officials of the surrender committee. Greater duty to the whole demanded his presence at this moment. His eyes fell in defeat, seeming to realize some headstrong individuals needed to be the masters of their own fate. He shook his head and waved for the confused sentry to lower his weapon. The gate immediately creaked open and Mrs. York stomped through, with her brood filing behind her. A few other families scrambled behind her, but Denison did nothing to stop them. The gate creaked closed again, much to his relief.

"Come gentlemen," he said, turning towards the stunned officials. "We have larger fish to fry at the moment."

Everyone followed them to the north gate and watched them march through it. It creaked closed behind them and most folks collapsed in exhaustion. It all seemed too much. How much more could we stand? seemed to be the question on everyone's mind.

Many prayers followed the surrender party on their loathsome march to the remains of Fort Wintermoot, but few eyes watched them from the walls. Now everyone lay their fate in the hands of Providence. Our lives now lay in his hands, and only he could save us, we all felt certain of it. The failings of man never seemed so clear to me as then, though only a child. And the cost of liberty never seemed so stark as then. Never!

Chapter Nineteen

The flies buzzing about, the ceaseless groans of the wounded, the stifling heat, the growing noxious odors, and the uncertainty of our fate, made Forty Fort a horrible place. It seemed everyone had gathered here, and the few whom had departed so suddenly seemed not so foolhardy. But beyond that, a love for our land kept each of us in place.

People muttered their prayers unceasingly, but also reasoned and hoped among themselves. How could Indian Butler not abide by the rules of civilized society? How could he let a massacre of women and children occur, after all, even tyrants had their standards. Someone held his reins. His actions had to be accounted for. Butler would be hated and hunted by both sides if he allowed the slaughter of innocents, no matter how misguided.

I and Will sat huddled together watching it all, trying to force our tied eyelids open when they felt so heavy. Our youthful exuberance would not allow us to miss anything. We watched the slowing pacing widows, still crying and wailing something fierce. Oddly, their scratchy wails almost seemed normal and we almost grew accustomed to them. Strange, that horror should ever become so, but it did. It got so bad some folks cared not where they defecated, so distraught they had become, especially the children, for their mother's grief numbed them so. Our home slowly started becoming a living nightmare, a dream turned sour in more ways than one.

When my eyes finally fell closed a commotion to the north gate immediately forced them open. Will perked up and ran to the crowd assembling by the gate. I started to rise, but suddenly fell back down, tired as I was. Only with the most extreme exertions did I force my body up, and my young, but tired muscles, did ache. But I must see!

I grudgingly stumbled to the rear of the parting crowd. Leaning on the nearest leg, I watched Denison and his party despondently step through the crowd, a few of them stammering and mumbling an explanation to the anxious people hovering around them.

Finally one rather gruff soul demanded, "Speak up you damn fools! Our hair hangs in the balance, too!"

Denison suddenly stopped and turned towards the gruff soul, his eyes glaring wide. He gritted his teeth and shook his head. An expectant hush fell over the crowd.

"They'll be here soon," Denison yelled, raising his hands high. He slowly turned for all to see him. He locked eyes with many throughout the crowd, and I swear I noticed a glint of a tear in his stern eyes. "But the terms are most favorable, as they are now, at least," he continued. "Each man shall remain in possession of his property and land and are not to be molested, that is if he swears to keep out of the festering conflict with England! They shall be coming soon to formalize the treaty, if not only to gloat!"

Denison's tongue fell silent, and no one spoke for the longest moment. Everyone stood aghast and watched their leader's crestfallen head fall to his chest. His high hands also fell, and he stood silent, an embodiment of all our feelings. No one argued, for they knew this man had done his best, and none among them could do better. The Lazarus Stewarts of the crowd all lay silent and tortured on that horrible field or had hastily departed the valley, only the reasonable remained. The reasonable and those humbled by their great defeat.

John Franklin, arriving too late the day before to march into battle, took over for his crestfallen commander. He barked this order and that to the stunned crowd and he himself helped usher Denison to his cabin.

Doctor Gustin, forsaking the strong sense of vanity of the times, rolled his sleeves up exposing his white skin, and drew his spectacles from his pocket. One rarely witnessed such actions, for rather than what the popular man of the day may think of his pioneer forefathers, they were a rather vain people. One rarely went without a shirt, for the sign of white skin, the whiter the better, showed the man need not toil in the fields to survive; as the so-called Rednecks did from breaking their backs in the fields. And the wearing of spectacles was completely frowned upon, and once during those days I heard tell of a fine gentlemen in Philadelphia whom had the nerve to use a new invention, an umbrella, in a pouring rain, for which he was so belittled the word stretched clear to the frontier. Beards were quite out of fashion, also. It was indeed a clean-shaven time, even on the frontier. I remember hearing of how Beth Jenkins blanched upon sight of a bearded Johnny when he made good his escape. One would think such curiosities of civilized life would be forsaken on the rough frontier, but I assure you such was not the case. I rarely saw Grandpa draw his spectacles, but in the dead of night when the doors were closed from prying eyes. He would rather squint and feign indifference when a paper was presented to him in public, rather than show his need for spectacles. The more times change, the more they remain the same. Such is the vanity of man.

A few men, such as Doctor Gustin, ignored such things now. Practicability demanded it. Though I have no doubt some men, and women, would have rather died than forsake their proper manners and ways. But not Doctor Gustin. He waved his hands to and fro to his friends and people helping him tend to the wounded. Oddly, Hooker Smith went about his duties without so much as a questioning look to his fellow doctor, also his son-in-law. Perhaps the dread of their tasks overcame their curiosity.

I and Will watched them gather what meager supplies remaining to them and rush them into a nearby cellar, madly urged on by the waving doctor. "Come now," he said, "we must have something hid for the poor wounded, for I take little stock in any treaty with those fiends!" He glanced over the spectacles dangling at the end of his nose to I and Will and our eyes widened back to him. "Come on boys," he said, waving towards some nearby bundles. "Grab what you can, boys, for we need all strong hands just now!"

We both scampered to him and grabbed what we few

things we could manage, passing them along to the eager hands of the men standing in the cellar door. We grunted and pulled, but showed ourselves equal to the task, and beamed with pride when the good doctor patted us on the heads and smiled at us at the end of our task. The sweat cut streaks through the blood on his grinning face and upon feeling his sweat-soaked hand on my shoulder, I looked to see red on my shirt. Along with the biting flies, swarming mosquitoes, and rancid stench, I shall never forget those days, for the high emotions of terror forever etched them in my mind.

Being relieved of our task by a the bloody, but grinning and appreciative doctor, I and Will found ourselves drawn to Franklin's men stacking the forts' firelocks in the center of the fort. Many a crestfallen and downcast man from the wall stumbled up and reluctantly surrendered his firearm, his last symbol of resistance, to Franklin's men. One group, led by Roswell Franklin, the only surviving officer left in the Hanover Company, refused to give up their weapons and the ensuing tumult brought Colonel Denison forth.

After speaking to a very agitated Franklin for a few moments he turned and waved his hand to the south gate. Roswell Franklin nodded and immediately scampered through the opening gate. His men followed Indian file behind him. Not all could surrender their hopes, it appears.

Undeterred, John Franklin continued his unsavory task. The grim look in his and his men's eyes spoke volumes of their true feelings. I watched them all gaze mournfully at Roswell Franklin's men exiting the gate, wishing for all the world to go with them. But duty sometimes demands such, and these men did not flinch from duty. The Hanover men always had a streak of independence beyond all measure, anyways. Known throughout the colonies as great Indian slayers, perhaps Colonel Denison felt it prudent they depart, also.

Chapter Twenty

Then they came. A forlorn call from the north gate announced their advance. I have never felt such a hollow and empty feeling, and can tell you everyone shared the same feeling. Everyone's face drew sour. They had struck a bargain with the devil, and now found it impossible to rescind. The horrible die had been cast.

Even those whom somehow kept faith in the whole affair suddenly blanched. Some women collapsed to the ground, wringing their hands and crying mournfully for their dear husbands to somehow protect them from the grave. Younger women, with husbands in the wars, such as Ma, strove to console the other mothers, but dropped into silence with vague words on their quivering lips. None, save the men already about the walls, climbed the ladders to look down upon their tormentors. Their imaginations drew their own stark and fearful images in their minds. They need not eyes to see it.

Denison, swallowing hard to erase the contemptible look about his face, straightened his fine hunting shirt and fine beaver-skin hat with a large feather sticking in it, and strode towards the gate, waving his hand fleetingly in the air for the gate to open. Captain Franklin followed at his heels, with everyone else skulking down along the sides of the fort near cabins and such to quell their fear. But all knew if they even did mange to barricade themselves in the cabins it would be only a matter of time before the doors burst open from gruff British and Indian hands. There truly was no escape. Many stood stoically and muttered prayers through quivering lips.

The gate creaked open, with a slow grinding noise that scratched into each and everyone's soul. There they stood, all rigid and proud, their glaring eyes looking forwards in a strange awe. No one, on either side, spoke for the longest moment. On the left stood Indian Butler himself, all plum and proud, grinning like a stuck pig in front of his green-coated legions. Behind him fluttered that awful flag which had once flown with pride over our whole land, but now flew over heads filled with utter distain for it and all it represented. To the right stood their dark-eyed allies, all painted and decked out in their beaded and bright clothes, grinning and staring with an awful look of anticipation. One of their queens stood to their front. Behind her barrel-chested chiefs stood, jutting their chests' proudly. Their dark eyes glared with utter contempt.

Indian Butler seemed to almost immediately notice the look of shock on our faces and smartly raised his hand. A pair of fifers behind him raised their instruments to their mouths and drew a deep breath. The drummer to their side raised his drumsticks high, ready to bring them down when Butler's hand fell.

Denison suddenly strode forth, nodding his head and waving towards Butler. Butler stood stunned for a moment. His hand froze in the air. The fifers and drummers stood still.

Denison nodded, but before the stout British major could speak another voice scratched through the silent air. "Den-i-son!" the Indian queen screeched loudly. "You make me promise to bring more Indians to trade!" She slowly turned and spread her hand to the great painted hordes in her wake. "See! I bring all of these!"

"That woman should be seen and not heard!" Indian Butler immediately said, turning a cold eye to the stoic chiefs behind her.

They glared at him without a word.

In a huff, Butler smartly lowered his hand before Denison. The fifers and drums immediately struck up and played. The sharp shrill of those fifes still etch their way down my spine, even after all these years. I hope America shall never have to hear John Bull's shrill tunes on this soil again, for they counter all which we stand for in this world.

Butler stepped forward and the whole menagerie stepped forward behind him. His smart soldiers marched to the left and the Indian hordes flowed through the gate on the right. A collective gasp rose from all of our throats. Now it truly had begun. I know I for one glared at the dark eyes of the Indians and down to their tomahawks and knives tucked in their brightly colored sashes. I remember shrinking in fear, suddenly seeking out Grandpa and Ma. I found them in front of our cabin, their mouths agape and staring gauntly at the invading hordes. Will shrank behind the folds of our mother's dress, peeking out from the folds every now and then. I grabbed the other side of her dress, feeling no shame in it in the face of the horrors descending upon us.

Both of the parading parties fanned out around the stacks of firelocks in the center of the fort. Butler, spying the beaming eyes of the Indians, promptly stopped his men and motioned them towards the weapons. The Tories immediately seized all the arms, taking them up under the suspicious eyes of their painted allies of the unforgiving forest.

Butler, reconsidering his harsh actions, suddenly ordered all his men to lay down the captured arms. Coldly watching his disgruntled men slowly respond, he patiently waited for the last of the muskets to fall to the ground.

The chiefs watched his every move and two of them stepped towards the plump and haughty British officer, but Butler stopped them short with a cordial wave of his hand. "See brothers!" he yelled, slowly turning and spreading his hand towards the pile of weapons, "the Yankees, they give you all of these as presents!"

An immediate tumult broke out among the Indians. They crowded and swarmed around the pile of weapons, raising this one and that one up in the air in triumph and passing them around until a certain satisfied soul claimed it. Their screeches and yells filled the air, and our souls with fear. Oh, how they knew how to intimidate a person. I can only imagine the horrors Johnny and other poor captives had to endure amidst their number with no hope of escape. Such horrors indeed!

The Indian queen, seeming not so easily appeased by Butler's gesture of good will, stomped up to Colonel Denison. The bells about her dress and moccasins jingled with each of her forceful steps. Her eyes glared at Denison, seething with anger. She stopped just short of him and eyed him up and down with her dark eyes. Finally, she took a brave step forward and snatched the feather from Denison's fine hat.

Denison jerked back, but too late.

The queen turned towards her minions, grinning from ear to ear and holding her prize high in the air. Her actions immediately incited many copycat actions. Many of the Indians scattered among the crowd, searching their persons and taking whatever caught their fancy. Some of the odd fellows shook each of the stunned settlers' hands, swearing "Goot, goot friends now!" The odd gesture drew the ire of some, and the distain of all, but we had to endure. We had no choice.

Butler coyly ushered Denison aside, mumbling something in his ear to draw his attention away from his strange allies. They soon stomped towards Thomas Bennett's cabin, there to disappear for quite a while. The men of the surrender committee quickly joined them, along with Captain Franklin, three green-coated and stuffy officers, and an equal amount of chiefs.

The shaking of hands soon ceased and plunder of all sorts began flying about in tawny hands. They all smiled so and raised certain pieces of plunder, once our prized possessions, in our faces, shaking their heads at the cold eyes staring back at them. They genuinely seemed unable, for the life of them, to understand our ire. To them, they had won and now enjoyed the fruits of their victory. It befuddled them that we did not share in their happiness. Such were the differences totally opposite cultures produced.

But soon the savages, decked out with the stolen finery taken from looted chests and from some people's very backs, parading about trying to imitate our manners, provoked a few smiles even amid the great sadness they caused. A ruckus in one of the cabins soon drew our attention and people crowded around, both white and red.

A stubborn red-headed woman sat atop a chest with her arms folded. A young and infuriated brave demanded she get up, but she steadfastly refused. Locking her eyes to the floor, she put her palms to her ears and sat, much to the brave's growing angst. He stomped out of the cabin and parted all of us gawking at the spectacle. He quickly returned with an older warrior brandishing a tomahawk. To our gasps, he bandied the deadly weapon about her head, but she sat stubborn and fast. His scream caused many of the young woman's friends to plead with her to desist. Her stubborn behavior might invoke a frenzy among the swarming savages and then they would slay us all, they pleaded.

Shaking her head, she finally rose. The angry braves pushed her aside and screamed in triumph. Indian women scrambled to the door. Soon the chest flew open and all of the young lass' garments graced many Indian women's person. They seemed giddy with enthusiasm and immediately cloaked themselves in the fine dresses in any manner, some putting on one garment after another. A tower of bonnets sat high atop one of the grinning Indian women, all backwards and bobbing with each nod of her head to her fellows.

The braves rambled through the rest of the cabin, very indifferent to the sad eyes watching them and the sobbing young woman. They screamed again in triumph and lifted several feather beds. Tumbling through the door they immediately engaged in their most favorite and odd habit of slicing the beds open and flinging the feathers high in the air. Their dark eyes sparkled as they watched the multitudes of feathers dance in the air and float on the breeze. One after another feather bed fell to their hands, spewing feathers everywhere. They ran with glee to the river, flinging more of the feathers onto the water. Their antics did seem so odd and almost comical in retrospect, but not at all at the time.

Their odd fascination with the feathers did offer some relief to us anxious children, though. At the behest of our parents, us children engaged in a little game to spite the tawny fiends. We secretly gathered many of the settling feathers in the wake of the frenzied Indians and saved them, tucking them into our shirts and such until we could deposit them in certain places. Doing such, the Gore family did manage to make a bed from the feathers after the ordeal, making the famous Wyoming bed, which I think still is around to this day. Oh, to see it again, a record of our little act of defiance in the face of impossible odds. It meant a lot to us then, and does to this day.

I will never forget stumbling about, my hands grabbing wildly at feathers, when suddenly I hit something hard. I fell, my darting eyes looking up through the swirling feathers to a pair of glaring eyes shining through them, locked right on me! Will screamed at my side and stood deathly still, watching me frozen with fear and glaring back at the Indian.

I suddenly recognized the eyes as belonging to no less than Black Henry himself, our former prisoner. He bared his teeth and snarled at both of us, sending us scrambling and reeling into the nearest dark corner. We stood there watching him laugh at us, but his attention soon turned to some braves gathering around him. I recognized one of them to be his partner whom had been imprisoned with him, and watched as he pointed to his fingers and grimaced, no doubt telling of his torture at the hands of us Yankees. It may seem foolish, but I guarantee no one who ever had his fingers slammed in a door will argue, having one's fingertips pinched with bullet molders does hurt, but apparently not enough to loosen an Indian's tongue.

More yells sounded beyond and soon Indian Butler himself strode by us. We rose and followed, drawn to his dark presence. He did carry himself well, strong and stern, as a man certain of himself and his actions. Some call it arrogant, and I will not disagree, though I have no doubt he would disagree.

He walked past a grieving woman collapsed on a bench with a small girl lying with her arms over her lap. The girl looked up at him. Her deep blue and bloodshot eyes widened and the tears running down her crimson cheeks poured all the more. "Mommy," the girl muttered, locking eyes with the British demon, "how could such a fine looking man bring the Indians to kill us all?"

Butler blanched at the words. His eyes suddenly widened and he shook his head. Turning, he announced loudly that we Yankees had brought all this about ourselves and that if we would have remained peaceful and not sent food and men to the Rebel army, none of this would have ever happened.

No one replied to his proclamation and he strode towards the north gate in a huff, glaring back a warning for I and Will to get if we knew what was good for us. We both scampered back towards our cabin, there to find our weeping mother trying to console our crestfallen grandmother. Grandpa stood with a stunned look and with his jaw agape, as an Indian had just relieved his jaw of his prized pipe. I swear he was fit to be tied, but held back his rage, knowing it would go for not.

We then heard the distinct report of a half dozen rifles at the north gate. I can never forget the heartrending sighs and sobs at the sounds of those guns completing the work of death. We all stood breathless for the longest moment afore word passed from settler to settler that Indian Butler had recognized Sergeant Boyd, a British deserter whom helped train the men of the Twenty-fourth, and had him quickly shot by Indians. Another brave Wyoming soul lost to the ages.

With gasps following his every step, Butler strode to the middle of the fort. Looking to the waning sunlight and his whooping allies, he called his troops together and marched out the north gate, caring a throng of still celebrating Indians in his wake. They herded all our animals among them. I scorned them for that, thinking of the milk of cows. Mush and milk was a staple. But we all scorned them more as flames started rising in the sky from the near cabins in their wake. It started, the flames of our doom.

Thirty or so stayed behind, both rangers and Indians, no doubt to keep an eye on us.

One reluctant Indian rode among the departing

Indians. As she grew closer I recognized her face all scrunched up under a dozen towering bonnets as the queen. I had to take a second look as the many captured petticoats she wore, one atop another, made the small-framed woman appear plump. I was told she was none other than Queen Ester herself. This drew my stare all the harder to her. The sight is still engrained in my mind, for she seemed so odd, almost childlike, despite her high position and social stature. She was Indian, true to the bone, no matter what others say these long days past.

I have heard people argue in these days, clouded by the haze of time, that it was not Ester upon that bloody rock. By I myself saw crestfallen Hammond, and he glared at her with eyes so full of hatred as she passed I feared his bulging eyes to burst. He had been about that rock the night afore. He had barely escaped, but through a great heroic effort of he and Elliot. Both swore to their dying day it was Ester, and what with Colonel Denison recognizing her along with Captain Franklin and scores of others, including Major Butler himself, I believe that gloating Indian, I myself witnessed long ago, to be no more than Ester herself. As for the argument of the Indian woman witnessed at the fort being plump, and Ester being known to be slight of frame, the many captured petticoats explain the mistake. I swear she wore so many towering bonnets her face dripped with sweat under them. And those grizzly scalps she help in her hands only attest to the fact. She displayed them full and strong, seeming proud of exacting revenge on the hated Yankees for killing her son afore the battle. I believe he to be one of the braves our brave soldiers dispatched when they went to relief of the Harding party afore the battle proper.

Besides, the way the Indians paid her homage, it could be no other. Why would they let any other woman ride at their head as they triumphantly entered the fort? Ester was the Queen of all about Tioga Point, nothing happened without her sanction along the Susquehanna there abouts. Thus I hope to settle the question, in my mind, anyways.

Chapter Twenty One

The light of day did shine the next morning, despite our foreboding sense of dread and I arose from my fitful slumber to greet it, hoping the night before to be but a nightmare, but alas, it was not. I looked down at Will curled up tight next to me in the crowded cabin and rose ever so slightly, as not to disturb him. We all had such little sleep these past days.

Scared, huddled, and shivering, I sat all night, watching my crying mother and forlorn Grandparents. All of the world seemed to collapse. Indian yells echoed through the cabin all night and I did so wish for my brave Pa to come back from the war far away, for it had come right to his home, and threatened his entire family! All of us were gripped with fear, fear of everything. I can still see that dark fort in my nightmares to this day. The Indian yells did not end all the night, nor all the rest of my life. They haunt me to this day. I remember, but wish I did not. Thus, I write this *page in time* to relieve my mind through recollection. I must do something.

I gazed about the cabin to the people crowded everywhere, all in a restless sleep at best. A few forlorn women sat upright, their blank eyes staring out from the nothingness in their souls. Their bloodshot and tired eyes betrayed their empty hearts, emptied by the horrors of war, and the great sacrifices of their dear husbands, fathers, and sons. It made me shudder and I wished to lay back down and gain what reprieve I could in my fitful sleep, such as it was, but the rustling noises outside the cabin drew the bane of all young boys, curiosity, out of my me. It drew me up and past the trance-like widows to the door, there to greet the horror again.

Indians sat scattered about, starting fires and partaking of our captured food. They still seemed jovial and I think the thrill of their victory kept them awake all night, also. But they did behave, such as an Indian could, and showed great restraint.

Glaring eyes of the their fellows, blue-eyed Indians, shot to me in the door and I reeled back from their hateful stares. Their eyes bore a greater hatred than the now appeased Indians, and in that moment I feared them more. Their eyes shot arrows of hate straight and sure.

A group of painted Indians all bunched around a great barrel-chested chief passed through the hateful stares and I followed them, curiosity drawing me along. They had discovered some of the cellars by the cabins and split off from the group as they advanced to search each one. The chief, leading the remaining few forward, marched directly towards the sloping cellar door by the makeshift hospital.

Doctor Gustin suddenly appeared from nowhere and quickly interceded between them, stopping their march for a moment. He spoke to them in English, and seeing the odd stares his words caused quickly switched to French, which drew their attention. They talked back and forth in the poetic language for the longest time with the chief finally pointing over his shoulder. With his other hand he waved a brave forwards towards the door, despite the doctor's protests.

Doctors Gustin's eyes suddenly drained and his faced blanched. He almost collapsed in grief when another of his party burst forth and stopped the brave, waving his hands and saying the one dreaded word which all knew, in any tongue, "Pox! Pox!"

The brave immediately reeled back and retreated from the door, his eyes wide and full, as if he had narrowly avoided a leaping catamount. The chief looked up to the stunned and suddenly reanimated doctor and asked, "Pox?"

The doctor nodded his head profusely and sighed as the chief waved everyone back away from the door. They soon became lost in the new plunder pulled from the other cellars. All but one. An old Indian woman with a deeply wrinkled face and long, dirty fingernails, advanced headlong towards the door carrying a small bucket, much to the good doctor's angst.

The doctor quickly interceded but the woman brushed him aside. The doctor raised his hand as if to hold her back, but reconsidered, noticing some of the braves watching him.

He pulled his hands back and slumped his shoulders, running a hand through his hair. He stood tall again as the old woman simply dabbed the door with some black paint.

He smiled and nodded to the old hag as she backed away cursing the crazed white devil in her native tongue. The strange and fast guttural sounds rolling off her tongue truly conveyed her ire, no matter the language.

It didn't seem to matter to the grinning doctor, though, for he smiled and nodded at her biting tongue. He turned and gratefully shook the hand of his quick-thinking fellow. He had saved their meager stores for the wounded.

I backed away to one of the nearby Indian fires and watched them sup with envy. My burning stomach ached for mush and milk, but knew I would have none this day. The indifferent eyes of the Indians showed no mercy for me. I collapsed to the ground and sat Indian fashion, watching the Indians feast, and yearned for them to just get up and leave, somehow thinking if I stared long enough at them with my unforgiving eyes they would do so. But, of course, it all was for not. I suddenly felt empty and a foreigner in my own land. The distant and multiplying smoke trails climbing in the sky over the fort's walls and the echoing cries of the Indians did little to ease my angst. All seemed lost. All seemed forlorn.

Ma soon grabbed me by my neck, yanking me to my feet. So entranced in watching the Indians I did not see her approach and for a moment struggled and twisted against her, until her stern grip tightened on my neck, that is.

"Oh, Ma," I cried, "I hunger so!"

She rolled her eyes to the nearby Indians and turned me about, passing me a biscuit from her apron pocket. "Don't eat it here," she whispered, find some dark corner away from them, or they'll have it fer sure!"

Looking to the tears forming in my eyes, she ushered me further way from the Indians' prying eyes and stood with her person shielding me from their dark eyes. "Eat, Little Mose," she whispered, "eat fast young 'un!"

I munched down my prized biscuit in no time and beamed up at my mother. She smiled and stroked my hair, pulling me close to her side. "You keep about the cabin and don't stray," she said. "And keep an eye on Will!"

I nodded and scrambled off, my stomach full and my lust for adventure renewed. I found Will munching on a biscuit in the cabin and told him to eat fast, lest the Indians come and snatch it right from his mouth. He looked at me in shock and the tears stared flowing. I shook my head, suddenly ashamed, and reassured him all would be fine, I was only kidding.

After Will bit the last of his biscuit I dragged him by the hand to the door, there to see a new parade. A new chief led another bunch of Indians into the gate. Oddly, a bunch of them started spreading out amongst us forlorn settlers, dabbing our faces with red paint. I held Will tight to me and watched them approach. We stood rigidly still while an gruff Indian slopped red paint about our cheeks. "Keep!" the old brave said afore moving on, "it save you from wild Indians! No wipe!"

We watched him go and cast our eyes to a large chief stomping across the green towards the cabin next to us. The Indian's eyes showed mean and we watched him stomp up to the door and slam it wide open to a sea of gasps within it. He stepped into it and I and Will waited anxiously outside the door, trying to listen to all the ensuing hubbub within the cabin. A few loud protests in both the Indian tongue and English crept through the door, along with a few clanking pots.

The door flew open again and I and Will scattered in the face of the gruff chief. His cold eyes rolled down to us and he snarled afore raising his hands high in his new hunting shirt. A fine hunting shirt with a fringed collar and cuffs, made of the finest linen. We had seen it before, on Colonel Denison, no less, and blanched at the sight of it on the painted and tattooed Indian's back. I must say some the Indians sure did favor tattoos, for some were tattooed from head to foot.

Indians whooped upon sight of their brave chief and his fine prize taken from the very back of the Yankee chief.

The chief slowly turned and acknowledge all of the praises of his bravery. He turned back into the door and snarled one more time afore sauntering away from the cabin.

Martha, our cousin, soon appeared at the door, breathing fire and swearing an eternal vengeance against all the heathen until her mother scolded her. She looked over to Grandpa and exclaimed they took the shirt right off Denison's back, but, she added, drawing Grandpa close, they managed to save the wallet in its pocket containing all Wyoming's money, with a little act of deceit, so they were not totally victorious.

Colonel Denison stormed out the door behind her, clad in a dirty shirt and swearing to give Indian Butler a piece of his mind. His head showed bright crimson from anger.

Thomas Bennett appeared behind him in the door and watched him stomp off shaking his head. "It is too late," he said. "It would behoove us all to depart at once, while the getting is good!" His eyes raised to the columns of smoke rising over the wall from beyond. "It is hopeless," he gasped.

Grandfather followed his eyes with his own and then looked down to us. We scrambled to him and each took a leg, hugging it tight. His hand fell to our heads and he said, "Perhaps it is best we get while the getting is good."

Ma and Grandma nodded their heads in our cabin door. All looked to the growing hordes of Indians clamoring through the gates. Perhaps the time to depart had come, afore things truly got worse, for our bargain with the devil soured.

The appearance of Indian Butler trailing behind a disgruntled Colonel Denison saying he could do nothing the Indians made up Grandpa's mind in an instant. "Gather yer things, Ma," he said to Grandma, "anything you can tote, for we's a leavin' fer sure!" He looked his to Thomas Bennett. They exchanged a few agreeing words and both soon appeared on the porch, loaded down with pouches.

They took one step from the porch when dozens of Indian hands twirled them about, stripping them of their pouches. They stomped back onto the porch. Kneeling down,

Thomas took a pouch from Martha and emptied it. Tucking in I and Will's shirts, he filled them with biscuits and such. "That's the way we'll have to do it," he said, "all of you tuck it into yer clothes, fer it looks as if we'll be lucky to get out of here with the very shirts on our backs!"

We all hastily complied and soon trotted towards the south gate in Indian file, easing our way through the swarming Indians. One stopped and twirled Martha about for a second, but her cold eyes turned him away and we continued on our trek, with Ma yanking I and Will along by the hand behind her. It was no time for play. Now it turned serious, and our very lives hung in the balance.

The passions of war twisted everything, and no sense of honor, tradition, or flag could save us now, but ourselves. I remember seeing their flag flying high over the fort as we scamper way for dear life.

The rag of the tyrant showed its true colors this day.

Chapter Twenty Two

My stark eyes locked on the river, staring at the body caught on a sunken tree. More and more caught my eye hastily trotting along the bank, pulled ruthlessly by my mother's hand clasped to mine. Will muttered a cry which found an instant reprisal from my mother's glaring eye. No, this was no time to be a child, or show any weakness.

We rambled along in Indian file, stopping when Solomon Bennett's hand rose in the air. We all scrunched down and kept perfectly still, waiting for the painted miscreants on the bank ahead to wander off to who knows what mischief. It only mattered that they missed us, and we them. We liked our hair were it was, atop our heads.

With a nod of Solomon's head we silently trotted down the bank, with Ma's death grip on I and Will's hands pulling us along. When Yarington's ferry came into view we all sighed in relief. The tough old bird still ran his vital ferry, the only link across the river from the west to the east.

Ma pulled us all the more, as the ferry started to fill with terrified souls. We all filed up to it, there to gain a quick nod from Yarington himself to board the crowded raft. Grandpa eased up to him and whispered they had not the fare, as the Indians had relieved them of all but a few biscuits tucked in our shirts, and Yarington shook his head at him.

"What man?" he gasped, tugging on the tow rope. "You think I would charge in such an emergency!?!" He nodded and cocked his wide eyes to the growing columns of smoke rising in our wake. They seemed to roll down the river, slowly ascending it. One home after another, Wyoming burned.

"You men lend a hand!" Yarington ordered all the nervous men on the dangerously overloaded craft. Quickly scanning the landing for anymore poor unfortunates, he ordered everyone to pull. A few men with long poles sank them into the water and tried to help pole the ferry along, but it did no good, too many people blocked their way. Several children sat with their feet dangling in the swirling Susquehanna as to make room. I and Will envied them, pulled tight to our mother with her iron grip. Playtime was truly over.

Each man grunted for all he was worth on the rope, yanking the craft, rather than pulling it, across the river. The rope wined in protest by Yarington said to keep pulling, he had it in his mind to get out of here after this trip anyways. He had done all he could do, he said, casting an eye to his own family waiting on the east shore for him. As soon as he landed this load, it would be the last. He had to make haste downriver while he still had his hair, he said over and over. God would have to protect the poor souls still in Forty Fort. The man's face contorted with pain and he gasped. That rope did burn the men's hands so, for there were not enough gloves for all, and it took a great effort to yank the craft against the waters.

Several bodies floated by us, rolling and tumbling in the strong currents of the Susquehanna. "God bless their souls," Yarington said, "for I have seen many such in these waters, poor souls."

We finally reached the east shore and everybody tumbled off the ferry without a word, or even a goodbye. Yarington waved his family onto the raft with what few others he had invited to join him and pulled his great long knife. He sliced the rope through and grabbed a pole, hastily poling the ferry turned into a mere raft downriver.

Ma pulled us along and we marched up the bank, there to meet this one and that one, all asking what was happening at Forty Fort and exclaiming Pittston Fort had been taken and Indians were seen about this side of the river.

"No doubt," Thomas Bennett said, nodding to the great flames in the sky from Wilkes-Barre. Nearby spine-tingling wails soon filled the air. They had arrived. Wyoming was truly doomed.

"What are we to do?" the stunned people asked with their mouths agape.

"Beat feet for Fort Penn or Easton!" Grandpa said,

waving us up the road. Solomon, though young, led again. He had proved his mettle against the Indians in the late battle and we would have no other in our lead. His eyes drew keen from the horrors he witnessed on that horrible field.

Onward we trudged up the road, as it was called, though merely more than a foot path, and disappeared into the shielding folds of the forest, so we thought. Passing an abandoned farm, Grandpa said was Bullocks, the last Wyoming house before the great swamp, we started running into all kinds women and children thronging the road, with an occasional man to advise. All seemed confused. Great shock and dismay showed in everyone's wide eyes. All stayed silent, lest any noise draw forth our enemies from the forest. Everyone looked to every crack of a twig or rustle in the bushes with great concern.

Towering hemlocks soon blanketing the sky above, casting us into a bizarre world of darkness. Though we knew the sun shined high above, even it seemed powerless to penetrate those great branches. Ferns blanketed the path on both sides of the tight road, crawling with rattlesnakes. I saw many scurry away in front of us on the trail, but no one seemed to care. We all focused on getting to Fort Penn on the Delaware River, many miles beyond.

The spooky forest spread out into a mire the further we trod. Thorny brambles soon dotted both sides of the dark trail and oh, how they tore and grabbed at our clothes. We stopped but once or twice the whole day, and then only long enough to scoop our hands into a small stream or nibble on a biscuit. Will cried but once, and after Ma bent down to him with her bulging eyes to tell him to hush or the Indians would get us all, we heard not another peep from him.

With the growing night darkening the strange forest around us, and the fear which urged us on fading with distance, we started to slow. Coming to a slight clearing along the road Solomon waved us to a stop, and after a long and careful look around motioned us down to the side of the trail. The stale and damp smell of rotting logs and moss filled the air. The cold, damp, ground soaked our ragged clothes, but we nestled down into a restless sleep, cold and with no fire, lest it draw the Indians. The horrible, unforgiving Indians.

Mosquitoes came out something fierce, some as big as a full-grown man's thumb, and everyone swatted and cursed them under their hushed breathes. Ma grabbed a branch and took to fanning it over us young ones to quell our tears. Oh, what a miserable lot we must have appeared, all huddled low beneath those ferns on that muddy ground, swatting ceaselessly at hordes of great mosquitoes and jumping at every snap of a twig. Soon the eerie howl of a wolf echoed through the dark forest and once the distinct cry of a catamount sounded but a few yards away from us in the dense ferns. We all jumped and the men lifted their meager knives, ready to fight whatever demon strode forth from the dark folds of the forest.

Latter in the night we heard another rustle and looked to see an old man and woman stumbling along through the ferns. Despite Grandpa's and the others' pleas for them to settle down and perhaps join us, they trudged onward, grateful for the biscuits we handed them, for they had only the clothes on their very backs and seemed so completely broken in spirit. I wonder of those poor folks to this day, and with a sad heart feared the backs of some dead folks we saw the next day along the trail to be them, God rest their souls.

The next day we finally emerged from the dark, swampy, hell and Grandpa told I and Will its name-*The Shades of Death*. Apply named, I must say.

We struggled on for a few more days, growing weaker each mile. We soon exhausted our meager supply of biscuits and took to eating whortleberries we found along the trail. Those red berries never tasted so good, manna from heaven. Many people tramped off the trail in search of food never to be heard of again. Odd little pine-bough huts dotted the trail every now and then, giving shelter to some poor woman whom had given berth along the way. I saw one pitiful woman carry her dead infant all the way to Fort Penn, cradling it tight in her arms as if it were merely sleeping, but her great tears betrayed her knowledge of its death. She said she just couldn't bare to leave it in the Shades of Death, it being all she had left of her family, for her husband perished in the battle. Such scenes were commonplace, and their horrors forever haunt my soul.

I often wonder of the will to survive, for I witnessed it full, especially on that horrible trek through the unforgiving wilderness to safety. Some people, shaking and stumbling all the way, made it to Fort Penn, while some more stout-hearted souls were never seen again. Spirit plays an important part in it all, despite the body's failings. Many died of hunger and exposure on that trek, I seen them. Others died of excitement and fatigue, and many simply never found their way out of the wilderness after they turned their backs on Wyoming. By what sufferings and tortures many died we shall never know, for hundreds perished on that cruel trek. Death stared everyone in the face upon every step. Some succumbed to its threat alone.

Captain Spalding did finally come, but much too late, but he did turn towards Fort Penn and relieve many peoples' suffering along the way with his soldiers' presence and their meager, but life-saving, stores they shared with everyone they encountered. Mathias Hollenback, that stout soul, rode on with his horse's back full of bags of biscuits to feed many along the trail, though gravely wounded. God bless him.

Then finally, after many days march, we climbed to the top of a ridge overlooking a beautiful glistening river, the Delaware, with great Fort Penn sitting atop its bank. Throngs of caring settles met us and ushered down into their fort, crying and urging us on, praising God that we had survived. All of the settlers running from the upper Susquehanna after that great invasion, on both branches, were met by helping and understanding people. It did unite us, if anything. Yankee and Pennamite lost their suspicion for that fleeting moment, and

New Jersey and New York offered a helping and understanding hand for all, helping their fellow Americans.

People say there were no caste systems then, at least for us frontier folk, and I say I must agree, though I also understand the cramped nature of the cities did breed another sort. A sort which found it a necessity for rigid social codes which, in my eyes, do more to separate than to unite. But such are some cruel hearted people, thinking they are elite to the sufferings of their fellow man and thus need to be shielded from them. They live on the backs of the less fortunate. But, unfortunately, such are the ways of the world. But nonetheless, for one shining moment we did untie to snuff out such beliefs, however brief. A tyrant, no matter of what government, will find no friend in Wyoming. I hope it shall always be that way.

I understand when many old folk say of the times-"these were the happiest days we ever saw." One neighbor envied not the another, but, on the contrary, did all in his power to encourage and help along. Such was the true, Christian life of the pioneers, in spite of our terrible struggles.

It is for you, now, our posterity, to carry on in that dim light of liberty glowing from afar in the distant pass. Stop and take a look at it, and you may covet it with a heart equal to it in its birth.

Such were the pioneer days of Wyoming, may we never forget them, and see in them a part of ourselves.

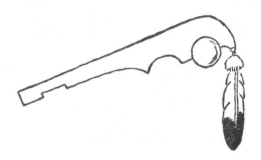

Made in the USA
Lexington, KY
13 November 2010